BETWEEN
HOPE AND HISTORY

ALSO BY BILL CLINTON

Putting People First
(with Al Gore)

BETWEEN
HOPE AND HISTORY

Meeting America's Challenges
for the 21st Century

PRESIDENT BILL CLINTON

TIMES BOOKS

RANDOM HOUSE

ISBN: 0-8129-2913-6

Composed by North Market Street Graphics,
Lancaster, Pennsylvania
Printed and bound by R.R. Donnelley & Sons,
Harrisonburg, Virginia

Manufactured in the United States of America

2   4   6   8   7   5   3

FIRST EDITION

*To Hillary, whose love, support, and example
have made my work possible and life joyful,
and to Chelsea, whose love and life remind me
every day of what all this work is for*

History says, Don't hope
On this side of the grave.
But then, once in a lifetime
The longed-for tidal wave
Of justice can rise up,
And hope and history rhyme.

SEAMUS HEANEY

Contents

Preface

THIS BOOK CONTINUES THE CONVERSATION I have had with the American people about our destiny as a nation, our duty to prepare for the new century, and our need for a shared vision of twenty-first century America that will enable us to grasp the extraordinary opportunities of this age of possibility.

The Proverbs teach us that "Where there is no vision, the people perish." I ran for President in 1992 because I thought that our nation lacked a unifying vision for our future and a strategy to achieve it, and that we were in danger of just drifting into the new era.

My vision for America at the dawn of a new century is of a nation in which the American Dream is a reality for all who are willing to work for it; our diverse American community is growing stronger together; and our leadership for peace, freedom, and prosperity continues to shape the world.

To achieve this vision we must pursue a three-part strategy. First, we must create opportunity for all Americans. Second, we must demand responsibility from all Americans. And third, we must forge a stronger American community.

In the three main sections of this book—Opportunity, Responsibility, and Community—I explore the most important challenges we face today, the progress we have made in the last four years and what still must be done, and what responsibilities individuals and families, businesses and labor, community leaders and government have as we move toward the next century. We know that when we stay true to our values and work together, America always wins.

I believe this is the path America must take into the twenty-first century. We have followed it for the last several years, and clearly it is beginning to work. We have 10 million new jobs; the deficit is down from $290 billion to $117 billion; our government is smaller by over 225,000 employees but is more effective; the crime rate has dropped steadily as we have put more police on the streets and taken guns away from felons, fugitives, and stalkers; our environmental and public-health standards are higher; our families are healthier and stronger. Still, there is clearly more to do. That is what much of this book is about.

But first we must make a choice: shall we live by our fears and define ourselves by what we are against, or shall we live by our hopes and define ourselves by what we are working for, by our vision of a better future. This is the choice that each of us—every individual, every family, every community, every generation—must make every day.

My balance scale tilts heavily in the direction of hope, just as America's does, and always has. We must be faithful to that tradition. If we are driven by our vision of a better future, we will achieve it.

BETWEEN
HOPE AND HISTORY

Introduction

HISTORY HAS A HABIT OF TESTING US—AS INDI-
viduals and as a nation—a habit of demand-
ing that we choose between our hopes and fears,
between our vision of how things ought to be and
an acceptance of things as they are. At 1:25 A.M. on
Saturday, July 27, a crude pipe bomb shattered
the night in Atlanta's Centennial Olympic Park,
killing one person, injuring scores more, and con-
trasting in an instant the best in the human spirit
with the worst. At a moment when the nations of
the world set aside their differences to celebrate
the Olympians striving for excellence, we were reminded that even then cowardice and viciousness
were alive, an ever-present challenge to our beliefs, our values, even our very lives.

In the hours that followed that tragedy, every
athlete, every team, every official, every individual

attending the Summer Games had to make a choice about how to respond. And when the sun came up, we all were witness to the greatest victory of the Centennial Olympics: the victory of hope over fears, of the eternal vision of the Olympics over terror. Every Olympic site was packed—with athletes ready to demand the best of themselves and with spectators ready to cheer them on.

The bomb, and the fear it created, did not cripple a people whose values are strong, blind those whose vision is clear, destroy the will of those determined to triumph. Instead, adversity reinforced our values, clarified our vision, and stiffened our resolve.

The Olympics presented America at its best, and the world the way we wish it could be every day. People from different nations, races, religions, and tribes, accepting the rules of the Games, respecting their opponents, reaching deep for the best in themselves. The Olympics also reminded us that even the best of times are vulnerable to the forces of destruction, then showed us how to respond to them.

History has often presented America with the choices of hope over fear, of lofty vision over adversity. In every age, Americans are required to meet the challenges history presents us and, as we do, to keep faith with both the values upon which our nation was founded and the hopes and dreams upon which people build their lives.

In our time, for example, leadership means standing with our allies to build peace in Bosnia, even though it places our own soldiers at risk. It means standing behind the forces of good will and peace-making in the Middle East, even after a brave leader like Prime Minister Yitzhak Rabin is assassinated. It means standing by such struggling new democracies as those in the former Soviet Union, even though we know progress will be uneven. It means standing up to terrorists and other forces of division and destruction, even as we mourn our losses and rebuild our lives, as we have in Oklahoma City. And it means standing firm, together, to ensure that our citizens, our families, and our children have the tools they need to make the most of their own lives, even though some would have us abandon that responsibility.

Our citizens always held America to the highest standards. And we have been richly rewarded for it. America is, and must always be, a place where individual dreams can come true, where people who work hard can succeed, where people of different points of view and different heritages can not only live together but prosper; a place where, by respecting our differences and working together to meet our responsibilities, we earn the gold medals of freedom and opportunity.

Nearly four years ago, I took the oath of office determined to ensure that America continued to meet these high standards. First, and most important, I wanted an America where the American Dream is alive and attainable for every single American willing to work for it. Second, I wanted an America that respects—even relishes—our diversity and builds out of it an even stronger national community. And third, I wanted an America that stays secure by remaining the strongest force for peace, freedom, and prosperity in the world.

For too long, American political debate had been polarized, stale, and often irrelevant to meeting our challenges. Citizens too often were forced to choose between two wrong arguments. One seemed to argue for the government to spend more money on the same bureaucracies working in the same way. The other argued that government was inherently bad and all our problems would be solved if only we could get government out of the way and leave people to fend for themselves. For the twelve years before I took office, this latter view dominated our politics, but was held partly in check by those who held the first view. What had this thinking yielded us? We were having the slowest job growth since the Great Depression. We had quadrupled our national debt in only twelve years. We were becoming more divided, racially and ethnically. And there was even some question of whether we had the will to support America's continued world leadership after the Cold War.

It was clear to me that if my vision of twenty-first century America was to become reality, we had to break out of yesterday's thinking and embark on a new and bold course for the future, with a strategy rooted in three fundamental American values: ensuring that all citizens have the *opportunity* to make the most of their own lives; expecting every citizen to shoulder the *responsibility* to seize that opportunity; and working

together as a *community* to live up to all we can be
as a nation. These three values have shaped the
character of our people and ensured our success
as a nation and our leadership in the world. They
are the basic bargain of America.

Most of us learn these values by living them in
our families, at school, at work, at our places of
worship, in our dealings with our neighbors and
friends. Most every American success story is a
tribute to their universal appeal. My belief in
them is rooted in what I saw and heard from my
mother, my grandparents, my teachers, pastors,
other caring adults, and friends; and later from
the Americans with whom I have worked and
have tried to serve, beginning in my native state
of Arkansas and continuing to this day.

Everything I have done in the nearly four years
I have been in the White House has been about
applying these three values—opportunity, responsibility, community—to meet the challenges we
face. At times of decision, I always ask myself: Will
this course give people more opportunity to make
the most of their own lives? Will it enable personal
responsibility among our people at home, at work,
as citizens? Will it bring us closer together, across
the lines that too often divide us?

These values determined my choice on perhaps the most contentious issue of the last year: the issue of how to cut the federal deficit and balance the budget. For nearly four years now, I have worked hard to forge a new consensus on a broad range of social and economic problems, including the need to balance the budget so that we can keep interest rates down and grow the economy faster, and not leave a legacy of debt to future generations. But a year ago that consensus was threatened by congressional budget cuts, which, in the name of balancing the budget, would have undermined Medicare, Medicaid, education, environmental protection, and the security of working families' pensions—all of which reflect the duties we owe to one another.

I am committed to cutting waste in government and balancing the budget. Our administration is the first to cut the deficit in all four years since the 1840s. We have cut it from $290 billion to $117 billion, a reduction of 60 percent. But I did not and will not permit passage of a budget that turns us into a country where the elderly, the poor, and the young are left to fend for themselves; that widens social divisions we have worked hard to close; or that hurts our people's ability to compete and succeed in the new world economy. In short, I vetoed the budget because it reduced opportunity, abandoned responsibility, and weakened our community.

For the same reasons I fought hard to save those programs, I have fought hard for programs like the Family Medical Leave Act and the Brady Bill, and against congressional efforts to repeal the assault-weapons ban, our program to put 100,000 police on the streets, our school anti-drug programs, our national service program, Ameri-Corps, and our environmental enforcement laws. The fight over these and other initiatives is fundamentally a fight over whether we will fulfill our obligations to each other, create more opportunity, and go forward together. These initiatives, and the commitments they represent, are safe for now, but they will only stay safe if we work together and keep faith with those values: opportunity, responsibility, community.

We live in an age of enormous possibility. But it is also a time of difficult transition. As we move from the Industrial Age into the Information

Age, from the Cold War to the global village, the pace and scope of change is immense. Information, money, and services can and do move around the world in the blink of an eye. There's more computing power in a Ford Taurus than there was in Apollo 11 when Neil Armstrong took it to the moon. By the time a child born today is old enough to read, over 100 million people will be on the Internet. Even our family cat, Socks, has his own home page on the World Wide Web. The opportunities this age presents us are extraordinary; more of our children will have the chance to turn their dreams into reality than any previous generation of Americans ever had.

But the challenges of this age are also extraordinary and the cost of failing to meet them is high. The actions we take today will determine what kinds of jobs Americans will have tomorrow, how competitive our businesses will be in the global economy, how well prepared our children—especially the poorest among them—will be to succeed, how secure and healthy our parents and grandparents will be, how safe our streets will be, how well we protect our land, water, and air, and how secure we will be as a nation in an increasingly complicated world.

These challenges are real and profound. Many of our cultural traditions seem under attack, sometimes from the very same sources of entertainment we often enjoy. Too many of our people, children and adults alike, are not getting the education they need to do well. We have access to more news and information than ever before but are often skeptical of whether what we hear is true, and that skepticism can lead to cynicism about whether our most basic institutions—especially our government—can work for us.

And elsewhere in the world, though the threat of nuclear war recedes, new threats abound. The very openness of our society makes us vulnerable to new forces of destruction that cross national borders: organized crime, drug cartels, the spread of dangerous weapons, including biological and chemical ones, and most of all, vicious terrorism.

Though the pace and perhaps even the scope of change in how we work and live, and how we relate to each other and the world, is unprecedented, our present condition has an instructive parallel in the not-too-distant past.

Almost exactly a century ago, America found itself in a similar period of profound, sometimes paradoxical change. As our nation made the transition from the Agricultural Age to the Industrial Age, vast numbers of people moved from farms to factories, from the country to the city, seizing new opportunities but also experiencing massive uprooting and dislocation in their way of life.

The very nature of work changed. People who had risen, worked, and rested following the cycles of the sun now punched time clocks—often day and night—and the conditions in many factories were often unsafe. Old work disappeared and new work emerged. The idea of community changed. With the advent of railroads and telegraphs, the small self-reliant town, often isolated both geographically and socially, found itself connected to the outside world. As cities expanded, as whole new urban neighborhoods grew and old ones were transformed, they throbbed with life, but many were also crowded, dirty, and unsafe. People became concerned with what they saw as the deterioration of moral standards and campaigned to shore up the values they felt were eroding.

A hundred years ago, the public demanded national action to deal with the challenges rapid change created. What emerged was the Progressive Movement. It was given voice and direction by Theodore Roosevelt, a president who was committed to ensuring that the free market worked for all Americans, protecting them from the abuses of the Industrial Age, conserving the nation's natural resources, reforming government, and asserting America's leadership in the world.

Theodore Roosevelt, and later Woodrow Wilson, went beyond the conventional thinking of both their parties. They were determined to use the power of the United States government to ensure that America secured the benefits of the new age so that our identity as a nation, our character as a people, the ideals expressed in the Declaration of Independence and the Constitution would be enhanced in the new era. The Progressive Movement was about a shared vision of what America could and should be, about mending the frayed fabric of family and community, about harnessing the forces of change and using them to meet both individual dreams and common national goals. That same shared vision guides us today.

In the face of bewildering, intense, sometimes overpowering change, people react differently. There are those who would try to avoid the future, to turn back the clock, or simply to hold out for as long as they can. And there are those who embrace the future with all its changes and challenges and engage in what Justice Oliver Wendell Holmes once called "the action and passion" of our time. The choices we make as individuals and as a nation make all the difference.

After each of the world wars in this century, our nation faced this choice—whether we would embrace or reject the future. After the slaughter of the First World War, we entered a time of wrenching change and enormous anxiety, a period in which the hottest novelist of the era, F. Scott Fitzgerald, said we grew up "to find all gods dead, all wars fought, all faith in man shaken." America withdrew from the world, seeking security in isolationism and protectionism. We withdrew here at home too, into the trenches of racial prejudice and bigotry and away from protection of our citizens and our economic institutions. Ten years later, in 1929, that decade of neglect produced the Great Depression. And soon thereafter, we learned we could not withdraw from a world menaced by dictators and found ourselves in a Second World War.

At the end of that war, we made a second, but very different choice. We decided to reach out to the future together—together here at home and together with the other nations of the world. In the tradition of Teddy Roosevelt and Woodrow Wilson, we embraced a view of ourselves and our democracy that Franklin Delano Roosevelt described as "built on the unhampered initiative of individual men and women joined together in a common enterprise." Abroad, we lifted former allies and former enemies alike from the ashes, and forged the institutions that enabled us first to contain communism and eventually to win the Cold War. At home, we invested in the future by investing in our returning warriors. We passed the GI Bill to help millions of Americans get an education, buy homes, and build the great American middle class. Those and other wise investments produced four decades of robust economic growth and expanding opportunity.

Today, at the edge of a new century, we face that critical choice anew: will we embrace the immense opportunities and difficult challenges before us or will we try to avoid them? Will we ensure all Americans have the skills and education they need to make the most of their own lives? Will we strengthen our families, protect our children, and ensure our parents and grandparents a decent retirement? Will we respond to the commercial forces that threaten the values, even the health, of our children? Will we leave future generations an environment cleaner and safer than it is today, or abuse it further? Will we continue to stand as the beacon of hope and a force for peace, or will we turn inward once again?

I believe we have learned the lesson of the past: we must embrace the future. We must meet the challenges of a new century and, at the same time, protect the values that have kept us on course for more than two hundred years.

It wouldn't hurt for each of us to keep our Declaration of Independence, Constitution, and Bill of Rights handy and look them over from time to time. The promise embedded in our founding documents is clear: America promises liberty, but demands civic responsibility. America promises the opportunity to pursue happiness, but does not guarantee it. To make good on those promises, we must provide the conditions and the tools which give all citizens willing to work hard and play by the rules the chance to make the most of their God-given potential.

That is America's promise. Today, as in the Progressive Era, we can redeem that promise only by embracing the future together, confronting its challenges together and seizing its opportunities together.

America has always held to a high standard. Our past was built on it. Our present grows from it. Our future depends on it. That standard is the ironclad commitment to three core values—opportunity, responsibility, community—that apply to all.

I

Opportunity

A T THE TURN OF THE CENTURY, IMMIGRANTS used to write to their relatives and friends back home that in America the streets were paved with gold. And in a way, they were. The real "gold" that paved our streets was the golden opportunity for people from any background to be able, through hard work and ingenuity, to make a fresh start in life.

The idea of opportunity has been a unifying force throughout our history. It draws out our best efforts. It draws others to our shores. And it draws all of us together in a common American Dream. It is the first part of the basic bargain of America.

Let me begin with a true story. In 1984, ten-year-old Marilyn Concepción's mother moved her family from Mayagüez, Puerto Rico, to

Providence, Rhode Island, in the hope of a better life for her family. Marilyn did well for a while, but after a few years of high school she dropped out. She took jobs in factories, movie theaters, delis—anything she could find. "I worked hard," Marilyn says, "but I realized my opportunities were limited." That's when she discovered AmeriCorps, the national service program I fought hard to create in my first year as President. "I was impressed with what I saw," she says, "young people taking an active role in their community." She applied and became an aide in an elementary school teaching English as a Second Language.

"Teaching turned me on to learning," Marilyn now says. After a month of studying, she became the first person in her family to earn a high school equivalency diploma, and today her older and younger sisters are following her example. Soon she was asked to join the AmeriCorps staff. Not long afterward, she was picked to help create a program like Providence's in San Jose, California. And last fall, at the age of twenty-one, Marilyn Concepción entered Brown University as a pre-med student. "Through AmeriCorps, I was able to help my community, my family, and myself," Marilyn says. Her hope is to return to her community as a doctor.

Our job as a nation, and indeed my job as President, is to blaze a path into the future by creating the conditions for economic growth that can benefit all Americans, and by ensuring that all Americans have the chance to seize the opportunities that growth creates. AmeriCorps, as Ms. Concepción's story demonstrates, is a symbol of what we must continue to do to build this nation: provide people opportunities, demand that they take responsibility for their own futures, and strengthen the community to which we all belong, because when everyone has a chance to live in dignity and succeed, we all do better.

That has always been the formula for success in America and embracing that formula has been the key to turning our country around. Let's recall where we were back in 1992. Unemployment was high. The deficit was at $290 billion and headed higher, and we had quadrupled our national debt in just twelve years. A rapidly globalizing economy demanded new levels of competitiveness from our companies, and some industries were struggling. The march of technology made new demands on individuals, especially for education and skills, but not everyone had those opportunities, and those who didn't were being left behind even when they were working harder and harder.

To restore opportunity, we had to reverse escalating deficits, spur economic growth, create jobs, and give people a chance to raise their incomes. Since I took office in 1993, I have pursued a strategy for expanding opportunity with three broad objectives: first, to put the nation's economic house in order so our businesses can prosper and create new jobs; second, to expand trade in American products all around the globe; and third, to invest in our people so that they all have the tools they need to succeed in the Information Age. The goal was clear: to prepare America for a twenty-first century in which we can compete and win as a nation, and in which every child—regardless of race, class, religion, or creed—can pursue a future in which the streets seem every bit as "paved with gold" as they were for generations before them.

To fulfill the first part of this opportunity strategy—putting the nation's economic house in order—we focused on cutting the deficit in half, bringing interest rates down, spurring private investment to fire up the nation's stagnant economy. The strategy succeeded. When I ran for President, job growth had been at the lowest level since the Great Depression, unemployment was nearly 8 percent, and the deficit was soaring out of control. After I was elected, we waged a brutal fight in Congress to pass a new economic plan. It passed by the narrowest margins in both houses, with no Republican votes for it and with Vice President Al Gore casting the tie-breaking vote, to get it passed in the Senate. Newt Gingrich, today the Speaker of the House, said, "This will lead to a recession." Richard Armey, now Majority Leader of the House of Representatives, said of our plan, "Clearly, this is a job killer." John Kasich, now Chairman of the House Budget Committee, said, "This plan will not work." Texas Senator Phil Gramm said, "If we adopt this bill the American economy is going to get weaker, not stronger; the deficit four years from today will be higher than it is today, not lower."

Well, three and a half years later, we didn't raise the deficit, we cut it by more than half. It was $290 billion when I took office and heading for $300 billion the next year. This year we will cut it to $117 billion. In fact, we would have a budget surplus today but for the interest we pay on the debt run up in the twelve years before I took office.

Cutting the deficit further until we balance the budget is vital to our future. The burden of this deficit drags us down today and jeopardizes our children's future tomorrow. Lowering it brings interest rates down so more Americans can buy homes and cars, start businesses, go to college, and build a better future for themselves and their families. But we do not have to sacrifice our future to bring it down.

That is what the budget battle of the last year was all about. At the end of last year and the beginning of this year, I waged a tough battle with the Republican-controlled Congress over the federal budget. Both the Congress and my administration had developed budget proposals with more than enough cuts to bring the budget into balance. The difference then, as now, is not in what to do, but how to do it. Their proposal would have dramatically cut needed investments in education and the environment and made massive cuts in Medicare and Medicaid. I believe, as I said in my State of the Union address, that the era of big government is over. But I do not believe that we can abandon our obligations to our children, our parents, and grandparents, or to future generations. That's why my budget proposal, which also eliminated the deficit entirely by 2002, did not make deep cuts in Medicare, Medicaid, education, or environmental investments.

The Congress was adamant about making these cuts, not to balance the budget but to advance their view that the market will solve our problems if we get government out of the way and let people fend for themselves. The market is a marvelous thing, but especially in a global economy, it won't give us safe streets, a clean environment, equal educational opportunities, a healthy start for poor babies, or a healthy and secure old age. The Republicans believed I would give in to them just to keep government going on a lot less money. But I wasn't fighting for "government." I was fighting for the future of America and for a different, less bureaucratic modern approach to help people help themselves. When I didn't cave in they shut the government down twice, and they hurt a lot of people. Eventually we got back to business again, and the debate about how to balance the budget goes on.

I believe more strongly than ever that the policy I have pursued is right for America. Let's look at the evidence. The fact is that today, as a percentage of our Gross Domestic Product, we have the lowest deficit of any major country in the world. As I said, had it not been for the interest we have to pay on the debt that was run up during the previous two administrations, we would have had a budget surplus.

And as for the economy, it is the healthiest it has been in thirty years, with low unemployment, low interest rates, and low inflation. We have 4.4 million more homeowners, and 10 million Americans have refinanced their mortgages at lower rates. Women and minorities own more businesses than ever before. And America has become the world's job-creation champ. From the beginning of my administration in January 1993, to the middle of 1996, our economy has created over 10 million new jobs, almost all of them in the private sector. Corporate downsizing in the last few years has received a lot of news coverage, and those who experience downsizing should get the support they need to resume productive careers. But, thankfully, we are creating millions of new jobs.

Several years ago, a lot of the new jobs being created paid below-average wages. That's not true anymore; in the last two years, two thirds of all the new full-time jobs created in the economy were in job categories that paid more than the median wage, and after a decade of stagnation, average wages finally are beginning to rise again.

With interest rates low and inflation at its lowest level since the Kennedy administration, American companies are thriving. In 1994, the World Economic Forum in Switzerland named the United States the world's most competitive economy for the first time in ten years. In 1995 they did it again, and pointed out that our lead over Japan and Germany was growing. Our exports are growing at record rates. Business investment is at a postwar high, and it shows. America's steelmakers are back, for example, with higher exports last year than any time since 1940. And after going for nearly a decade without hiring a single new production worker, General Motors added 4,000 last year. In fact, the Big Three automakers together will hire nearly 170,000 new workers by the year 2003 for good jobs paying good wages. America is once again the world's leading car producer.

As a result, for many Americans this is the best of times. But I am very aware that there are still too many Americans who are having a tough time, people for whom the gears of our economic engine don't quite mesh. Part of the problem is that what creates jobs and opportunity in America—at levels unapproached by any other nation in the world—is an economic dynamism that is inherently turbulent and disruptive. New businesses form and old ones die. New occupations appear and old ones disappear. New jobs are created and old jobs are eliminated.

Still, we have to face the fact that some of our fellow citizens who are more than willing to work hard and play by the rules are not being rewarded. There are basically three groups of Americans in this position. There are people who live in economically isolated inner-city neighborhoods and isolated rural communities that have felt no economic recovery because there are no new jobs there. There are people, principally the bottom half of America's hourly wage earners, who are working hard but aren't getting ahead because they don't have the kind of skills that are rewarded in this global economy. And there are people who have been downsized—many of them middle-aged—and it's taking them a much longer time to find another job with the same pay and benefits they were making before.

The answer to their difficulties is to get more growth, more high-wage jobs, and more education by building on the policies that have brought our economy back, with innovative, targeted practical efforts, not to abandon what we have done for a radically different course that will not help those who need it and will undermine opportunity for everyone else.

From the end of the Second World War through the mid-seventies, most Americans prospered. After that, and until two years ago, real wages declined or remained stuck in one place for most working Americans. Other kinds of compensation—health care benefits, company pension contributions, profit sharing—increased for some, but for many Americans the paycheck in the envelope at the end of the week didn't grow appreciably. And it didn't stretch as far as it once did, either; real purchasing power—our ability to buy things compared with what we're paid—eroded. For many Americans, the American Dream seemed to be drifting out of reach.

I believe American democracy cannot survive unless each of us has both the chance and the capacity to prosper. Americans don't resent successful people; we admire them. Resentment emerges in our society not when people who are successful have more, but when people who don't have much don't have a chance to do better. People want their own chance to do better; that's the core of the American Dream. And we have an obligation to ensure they have that chance, and the capacity to seize it.

Putting our economic house in order has gone a long way toward achieving this goal. So have responsible and targeted tax cuts in our economic plan, such as those for small business and the Earned Income Tax Credit, which is designed to cut income taxes for the hardest-pressed working families—15 million of them. It's worth about $1,000 to a family of four earning up to $28,000, and families get that cash even if their taxes were less than $1,000. The objective is to ensure that anyone who works full time and has children at home will be lifted out of poverty, not taxed into it.

In addition, we have taken steps to lift whole neighborhoods out of poverty through our Empowerment Zones and Enterprise Communities initiative. These efforts have channeled millions of dollars of new investment into neighborhoods and communities around the country that had been bypassed by economic opportunity in the past.

There is still more we can and must do to achieve more growth and more economic opportunity for working families. I have a balanced-budget plan with targeted tax cuts for America's families: a $500 tax credit, above the standard income tax deduction, for each of their children; more generous Individual Retirement Accounts with funds that can be used without penalty for important investments, such as buying a first home or further education, or even for medical emergencies; a tax deduction for the cost of college up to $10,000 a year, and a tax credit up to $1,500 a year for up to two years of community college.

If we look further ahead, it becomes clear that one of the key determinants of economic opportunity in the future will be the mastery of technology—by individuals and businesses alike. That's why I have fought efforts to reduce our investments in basic scientific research and development. Developing and, even more important, democratizing advanced technologies are critical not just to our national interest, but to every citizen of our nation. We cannot let this country be divided into technological haves and have-nots. We must make technology a force that serves rather than harms us, that unites rather than divides us as we enter the next century. We must make it a force that strengthens our ability as individuals and as a nation to adapt, compete, and succeed in the new era.

I believe that ten years from now, when we look back on this period, we'll see the passage of the Telecommunications Act as one of the most important contributions to democratizing access to technology in this country's history. It is a sweeping bill, one that includes not just the well-publicized V-chip technology to help parents screen out violent and other inappropriate television programming, but a wide array of provisions to extend technology into rural areas, into inner cities, into hospitals and schools. Even so, it is only a beginning.

We still have a lot to do before we can say all Americans have a chance to make the most of their own lives—but America is in better economic shape today than four years ago.

The second part of my economic opportunity strategy has been to help Americans take maximum advantage of global trade growth. The globalization of the world economy has had profound effects on work, on workers, and on wages. Money, management, and technology are mobile. Open markets mean products come into America that are made by people who work for wages Americans can't live on. This can cost some American workers their jobs and keep others from getting a raise.

But, overall, trade has brought vast benefits to most Americans. Hundreds of thousands of good American jobs are being created by the export of our airplanes, telecommunications equipment, food products, movies, and cars. And jobs in exporting companies on average pay considerably higher wages than jobs in companies that sell only within the United States.

If you listen to the trade debate that's raged during the last couple of years, you'd think there were only two approaches to the globalization of our economy. On the one hand, you have those who say we should just build walls around our country, keep out foreign products, and trade with ourselves. On the other hand, you have those who say what we need is pure free trade in which our markets are wide open to others and we hope they'll open their markets to us. Both of these positions are wrong. We don't need to build walls, we need to build bridges. We don't need protection, we need opportunity. But in a world of stiff competition we also need more than free trade. We need fair trade with fair rules.

That's why I fought so hard for the ratification of the North American Free Trade Agreement (NAFTA), which effectively opened Mexico's and Canada's markets to American products, and for the General Agreement on Tariffs and Trade (GATT), which is helping to level the playing field for American companies abroad. That's why we have worked hard, through the Summit of the Americas, to strengthen our trade connections in Latin America and to explore enlargement of the NAFTA membership. That's why we are working so closely with our Pacific Rim neighbors through the Asia-Pacific Economic Council (APEC) to make the most of that booming region of the world. And that's also why we and the other leading industrial nations work continuously to update international economic institutions, coordinate our economic and monetary policies and strike hard but fair bargains on the ground rules for open trade.

In all, during the past three and a half years we have negotiated more than two hundred trade agreements—twenty-one with Japan alone. In addition, in 1993 we created America's very first National Export Strategy and, more recently, a new agricultural trade strategy. And thanks largely to the leadership of our late Commerce Secretary, Ron Brown, we are working hard with American business leaders to open new markets for our products and our investments. The results? Exports have soared to an all-time high—indeed, just in the areas covered by our twenty-one agree-ments with Japan, exports have increased 85 per-cent, including cars, cellular telephones, even rice!

As a result of our efforts to create a new global trading system, the world isn't just a better place for Americans to do business, make money, and create jobs, it's also a safer place. The fact is that fair trade among free markets does much more than simply enrich America, it enriches all part-ners to each transaction. It raises consumer de-mand for our products worldwide, encourages investment and growth, lifts people out of pov-erty and ignorance, increases understanding, and helps dispel long-held hatreds. That's why we have worked so hard to help build free-market institutions in Eastern Europe, Russia, and the former Soviet republics. That's why we have sup-ported commercial liberalization in China—the world's fastest-growing market. Just as democracy helps make the world safe for commerce, com-merce helps make the world safe for democracy. It's a two-way street.

In the coming years, we will have to work hard to secure these achievements and build on them. We must continue to negotiate with our trade partners to lower trade barriers and insist that they play by fair trading rules. We must work to protect the global economy, and our own businesses, from fraud and instability in the trading system. And as we continue to work to open new markets, we must ensure the protection of our workers and our environment, as well as seek to advance labor and improve environmental conditions in developing countries. Our economic security depends upon it.

The third part of my opportunity strategy, and in some respects the most important over the long haul, has been investing in our people and our future—in research and technology, in education and skills, and in strengthening working families. In the rest of this chapter, I want to talk about each in turn, but together they really form a whole—a kind of "career tool kit" every American will need to succeed in the coming century.

The future prospects of average Americans today are being driven by one central force: rapid economic change—in *what* we produce (more sophisticated goods and services, less of some basic ones), in *how* we produce (more technology, less manual labor), in *who* produces (more skilled jobs, fewer unskilled), and in *how well* we produce (productivity).

The appropriate response to these changes isn't to cut investments in our future, as some Republicans in Congress advocate. The appropriate response is to *increase* investment in people power: by individuals in themselves, by private industry in its employees and production technologies, and by government in the basic building blocks of economic opportunity—education, training, and technology—so we can capture and share widely the benefits of this rapid change.

What kinds of investments? The kinds that help Americans today to succeed tomorrow. The kinds that equip our children to compete in the next century. The kinds that enable working Americans to weather uncertainty and profit from change. The kinds, in short, that ensure that all Americans have the capacity to make real choices.

Not long ago, I visited Union City, New Jersey, and saw the future. A city with a high immigrant population and many low-income families, Union City's schools were performing so poorly that the state finally threatened to take them over. But instead of giving up, instead of turning the task of schooling their children over to the state or to a private company, as some school systems have, Union City pulled itself together. The board of education voted to modernize, the city raised a new bond issue, and the state kicked in fresh funding. Teachers and other experts wrote new curricula for core courses and overhauled school management, giving schools more control over their budgets. The regional phone company, Bell Atlantic, donated computers and created media resource rooms. They also donated computers for homes and tied them into the school network. Parents came to school on weekends for training. Now they can keep in touch with teachers by e-mail and participate more directly in their kids' education. The result? Test scores and graduation rates are way up; truancy and dropout rates are way down.

Union City is using technology not just to strengthen school performance, but to strengthen the community as a whole. They are, in effect, democratizing technology, making it more readily accessible for children and parents alike.

But we will have to do more. That's why Vice President Gore and I are trying to hook up every classroom and library in the country to the Internet in the next four years. It's already under way. On March 9, we participated in a kind of electronic barn-raising in California, as schools throughout the state connected with the Internet. School systems did the organizing and parents did everything from raising money by selling cupcakes to painting school rooms after the wiring was done. More than a hundred high-tech companies throughout the state, including Sun Microsystems, Apple, MCI, AT&T, Netcom, America Online, Scholastic Network, Netscape, and Microsoft, contributed hardware and software, and the International Brotherhood of Electrical Workers and other labor organizations helped install six million feet of computer cable. That was only the beginning. In the months that followed, nearly one fourth of all schools in the state were wired to the Internet. And in another national initiative led by our administration, the national PTA, teachers' unions, and the National School Boards Association are helping to ensure America's teachers are as comfortable with computers as they are with chalk boards. In this "Twenty-first Century Teachers" initiative, 100,000 teachers will train 500,000 more teachers how to teach with computers, software, and networks.

But these innovations alone won't get the job done. At critical stages in our nation's growth we have had to raise our nation's educational norms to keep up with the demands of the times. We did it by making elementary education compulsory in the last century, by making completion of high school the standard in this century, and by making college available to returning veterans through the GI Bill.

Today it's time to raise the norms once again. We began that process in my home state of Arkansas in 1983, when I resolved, as governor, to make my state a leader in education reform. I created an Education Standards Committee, and after months of work and dozens of public meetings with parents and teachers who were pleading for help, we announced a comprehensive education reform program establishing standards for students, for teachers, and for schools. That same year the National Commission on Excellence in Education published *A Nation at Risk,* which warned of a "rising tide of mediocrity" in the nation's schools and called for our nation's public schools to undertake sweeping reforms to ensure that our children can meet the education and skill challenges of a new age.

In 1989, I and the rest of the nation's governors held the first education summit with President Bush. Together, we established broad goals for reforming education. We wanted every child to show up for school ready to learn, be proficient in certain core courses, excel in math and science, and graduate from safe, drug-free schools prepared for the world of work. We were convinced that the more you expect of students, the more they expect of themselves and the more they achieve. And we felt the same way about teachers and schools. If we expect more of them, and equip them to deliver, they will expect more of themselves and surprise us with their creativity.

This year the governors met again, this time accompanied by many of the nation's business leaders, to review progress and renew their commitment. In the seven years since the first education summit, over 60 percent of all four-year-olds now attend preschools; the number of young people taking core courses has jumped from 14 percent in 1982 to 51 percent in 1994.

National math and science scores are up a grade. And 86 percent of all our young people are completing high school.

The effort to create national standards specifying what students should know before they move on to the next grade, on the other hand, has had mixed results. Progress has been made with math and science standards, but efforts to create national history and English standards met with widespread criticism. This has shifted the focus of standard-setting to state and local officials, who, after all, have the primary responsibility for public education in the United States.

At the federal level, we have worked hard to help them establish clear standards for what we expect our teachers to teach and our children to know, assess their performance in attaining those standards, and ensure accountability when they do not. To help, we have marshaled resources, for example, to expand Head Start so that children come to elementary school ready and able to learn. I signed the Goals 2000: Educate America Act to help empower teachers, principals, and parents to change the way schools work—with cutting-edge technology, fewer federal rules, challenging academic standards, and increased parental involvement not just in schools but in their child's daily learning.

Now we must do more to make sure education meets the needs of our children and the demands of the future. First and foremost, we must continue to hold students, teachers, and schools to the highest standards. We must ensure students can demonstrate competence to be promoted and to graduate. Teachers must also demonstrate competence, and we should be prepared to reward the best ones and remove those who don't measure up fairly and expeditiously. In the same way we should reward the best schools and shut down or redesign those that fail, and especially those that are unsafe. That's one reason why I have supported expanding school choice and charter schools—creative new schools started by parents and teachers and licensed by school systems. And it's why I have announced a new $5 billion program that, together with state and local investments, will make a total of $20 billion available to renovate and modernize school buildings badly in need of repair—in inner cities, suburbs, and one-stoplight towns. We cannot build up our students if their schools are falling down, or their classes are overcrowded, especially as the largest class of students ever enters our schools in the fall of 1996.

We must also continue to rethink the roles schools can play in our communities. We are helping to expand pioneering "community schools" that stay open after three o'clock and are a community focal point for young people and adults alike. We must do more of this too. There will be fewer young people hurting themselves on the streets. In most states we are supporting school-to-work opportunities, designed with the business community, to create more paths to the future for young people not bound immediately for four-year colleges. We must do more of this.

Even a first-rate high school education isn't enough to succeed in today's economy. That's why I have been committed to carrying out a major "College Opportunity Strategy." One of the clearest messages our economy has sent in the last decade is that the one sure route to higher wages is higher education. And one of the clearest messages America's corporate leaders sent at the Education Summit this year was that they needed new employees with more education and skills than high schools provide.

I recall, as many of my generation do, how important the GI Bill was to our parents and our nation in helping create unparalleled prosperity in the postwar period. That's why, in this new era of change, I want to throw open the doors of higher education and opportunity to as many Americans as possible.

During the last three and a half years we have taken a number of steps to make college more accessible and affordable for more Americans. We have created a direct college loan program that cuts loan costs and offers students more repayment options, including repayment as a percentage of their income, so that no students will turn away from college for fear of being unable to pay the debt. We have tried, every year, to increase the Pell Grant program for people from working families. And of course, we passed the national service program, AmeriCorps, which has given nearly 45,000 young people a chance to work their way through college by serving their country and their community.

Still, I believe we must do much more. That's why I have called for the expansion of the College

Work Study program from 700,000 to one million students by the year 2000, and challenged colleges to use more of this money to put thousands of college students to work in community service. I have challenged high schools to encourage every student who can to do some community service and have offered to create $500 national service scholarships for high school students who have done significant work to help their community. In addition, I have proposed making it possible for Americans to be able to use their individual retirement accounts to help pay for college, and I want every student in the top 5 percent of every high school class to get a $1,000 scholarship.

These are important advances, but I believe that the facts of our time make it imperative that our goal must be nothing less than to make college available to all and to make the thirteenth and fourteenth years of education as universal as the first twelve are today.

To achieve this goal I have proposed two new tax cuts for American families. They are fully paid for by spending cuts in my balanced-budget plan. First, I have asked the Congress to pass a tax deduction of up to $10,000 a year to help families pay for the costs of all education after high school. And second, I have proposed a tax credit of up to $1,500 a year for the first year of community college or a four-year college, renewable for the second year if students maintain a B average or better, so that everybody everywhere can have access to at least two years of college. I call this tax credit America's Hope Scholarships.

These new proposals will open the doors of college opportunity to all Americans willing to work for it, regardless of their ability to pay, and make education and training available to every adult so that nobody will have to be stuck in a dead-end job. In short, they create opportunity so long as students take responsibility. These proposals renew the basic bargain that has made us a great nation and are critical to ensuring that Americans have the capacity to take advantage of the opportunities of the next century.

A minimum of two years of higher education will increase working Americans' chances of getting and keeping good-paying jobs. America cannot guarantee somebody the same job in the same company for a lifetime. That's not, and never has been, what our system is all about. But in today's turbulent economy, people have to know that if they work hard and play by the rules they will always have access to the training they need for new work. Thankfully most Americans live within driving distance of a good community college with an excellent record for placing its graduates in good jobs.

A short while ago, I got a letter from a man in his mid-sixties who lost his job four years ago at an aerospace plant and didn't know where to turn. But he wrote to us and we connected him to the kind of training program some in Congress are trying to eliminate and that man started his life over again, in his sixties. He is working again, has dignity, and is supporting himself and his family. This is not about big programs or yesterday's ideas. This is about equipping people to walk into the future.

I believe there is a national interest, and a national opportunity, in helping current workers broaden their educational skills and downsized workers go back to school—just as there was a national interest in sending Second World War veterans to college under the GI Bill. We have moved into a world where knowledge, which has always been a key to individual opportunity, is now the key to the success of the whole society and is literally the dividing line between those who can continue to do well for a lifetime and those who risk being left behind. We know today that every year of job training or further education beyond high school—whenever it occurs in life—increases a worker's future earnings anywhere from 6 to 12 percent. If we want Americans to earn more, we need to help them learn more.

America's best companies already understand this. Harley-Davidson, the company that brought the motorcycle industry back to America, understands it. They provide basic and advanced training in math, writing, and reading skills for all their workers at an on-site training center. Motorola runs its own "university." United Technologies will give its employees time to pursue another degree and help pay the tuition— whether the degree has anything directly to do with their job or not. They've realized that a better-educated employee is a better employee, period. Many other firms provide extensive and continuous training so their employees can move easily from task to task and advance to jobs with greater responsibility.

I have encouraged more companies to follow the example of the leaders in American industry. It's in their own best interest to do so. As Gerald Greenwald, CEO of United Airlines, said at a conference on corporate citizenship I called this year in Washington, "Every CEO in America says employees are our most important asset. Well, if that's true, why do we invest more in the overhaul of our machinery than we do in the training . . . of our employees?" I know many firms aren't big enough to afford sophisticated training programs. But I don't want their workers to be left behind, either, because I don't want America to be left behind.

That's why, for both downsized workers and for folks still working who know they need to strengthen their skills to get ahead, I proposed in 1994 and again in 1996 a new "GI Bill" for America's workers. The proposal was simple. First, consolidate some seventy overlapping, antiquated federally sponsored training programs and use the resources instead to support a simple $2,600 skills grant that workers can use as they choose for tuition or training. Second, give states greater flexibility to tailor training to employers' and workers' needs. Third, expand the network of One-Stop Career Centers already being created in the states to provide both existing workers and young people making the transition from school to work with information on jobs, careers, and the success rates of different training institutions.

The great French writer Anatole France once said the rich and the poor are equally free to sleep under the bridge at night. Even in a free society real choices exist only if people have the capacity to take advantage of them. I believe our job as a nation is to make sure Americans have the ability to make the most of their lives as individuals, as workers, as citizens of this great nation. And that means investing—wisely, but consistently—in education, in expanding college access, and in training and retraining America's workers. We cannot guarantee every American success, but we can make sure every American has a chance. Most of them will take that chance if we do. And if we do, we will all have more opportunity in twenty-first century America.

Along with a comprehensive overhaul of educational opportunity at all levels, we need to build up the security and safety of working families in the new economy by protecting their health care and their pensions. The opportunity to raise a family, care for your parents, and retire in peace all depend upon reforms that will ensure that workers won't lose their health coverage when they change jobs and that no company will be able to raid the pension funds of existing employees or limit the pension opportunities of new ones.

More and more people today are working for smaller companies that do not offer their employees health insurance, and partly for that reason, a smaller percentage of people in the workforce have health coverage than ten years ago. While Medicare takes care of Americans over the age of sixty-five, we're the only Western industrial nation that doesn't provide a system of health insurance for all working people under sixty-five.

We worked hard to create comprehensive health care reform early in my administration. And while that larger challenge remains unmet, we now have, thanks to bipartisan efforts, a new law that, among other things, ensures that people won't automatically lose their health insurance when they change jobs or when somebody in the family gets sick. That's an important new source of economic security for working families.

But we have more to do. First, we should provide assistance to unemployed workers to help them keep their health insurance until they find a new job. That reform is a part of my balanced-budget plan, but is not in the Republican one. We also need to make it easier for small businesses to buy into insurance risk pools that are large enough to make it possible for them to offer coverage at reasonable cost. Starbucks Coffee, for example, is a big chain today with some 15,000 employees around the country, but it hasn't always been big. Still, they've always provided health insurance for their employees. Why? Well, first, because they think it's the right thing to do. But it's also because they did a study and discovered that if they didn't provide their employees with health insurance the employees would leave within a year. And since Starbucks spends thousands of dollars to train every new employee, they simply couldn't afford that kind of turnover. Health insurance not only made their workers more secure, it paid for itself. This can have big benefits—not only for

employees, but for their employers as well. Sometimes it's possible to do right and do well, and we
should encourage that.

We should also encourage companies to offer
pension and retirement plans for their workers—
and protect the pensions of hard-working Americans from raids by their employers. Nationwide,
only about half of all workers have pension plans.
Three quarters of those working for businesses
with fewer than a hundred employees (the vast
majority of firms) have no pensions. That's not
good enough. We need to make it easier for
workers to set aside enough of their current income for retirement.

But that's only part of the problem. We need
to make sure that pensions are not at risk, either
because they are dangerously underfunded or because they are vulnerable to misuse by employers.
In 1994, Congress passed legislation I submitted
to protect the retirement savings of more than
40 million Americans whose pension programs
were underfunded or at risk due to mergers or
acquisitions. Since then, we've moved to protect
workers' pensions from employer fraud and
blocked efforts by the Republican Congress to

make it easier for employers to "raid" their employees' pension programs. And the minimum wage bill, which I recently signed into law, contains many of the proposals I made to expand pension coverage, portability, and security. It creates a voluntary small-business pension plan to make it easier for such businesses to provide their workers with pensions.

As with health coverage, when workers change or lose their jobs, they ought to be able to carry their retirement savings with them and keep right on saving. Today, not enough pension plans are portable and more and more people are changing jobs before they are vested in their pension. When American workers change jobs or are downsized out of their old job, they need to be able to roll over their old pensions into their new employer's program without a waiting period. So we're making it easier for employers to accept rollovers from new employees, and the new law contains my proposal to help eliminate the waiting period for new employees to start saving in their new employers' plans.

. . .

Naturally, it has taken time for this three-part economic opportunity strategy—putting our economic house in order, tapping the full potential of global trade, and investing in the capacity of our people—to translate into improvements in the bottom lines of average Americans. But it's happening. In 1994, the first year after my economic plan was enacted, family incomes increased across the board for the first time in years. Every family income group, from the poorest to the richest, had a real increase. Personal income rose 2.6 percent faster than inflation in 1995, continuing the trend begun in 1994. As I write this, wage growth is the fastest it's been in five years. Not surprisingly, consumer confidence has risen and the rate of home ownership has reached its highest level in fifteen years.

Our opportunity strategy is working. Now we have to build on it, to produce faster growth, more high-paying jobs, and more successful businesses. We can do that by balancing the budget to keep interest rates down, enhancing health care and retirement options for those who need them, opening more markets to our products, investing more in education, new technology and research, and targeting tax relief for education, child-rearing, and places where the economy is still weak. These measures will help more Americans help themselves, enable the economy to grow faster, and ensure that we will go forward together.

Some are offering a very different strategy, the same one they have offered before: an across-the-board tax cut bigger than we can afford. If implemented, it will either explode the deficit, raise interest rates, and slow the economy; or if it is paid for, it will require even bigger cuts in Medicare, Medicaid, education, and protection of the environment than the budget I vetoed. Either way, it will reduce opportunity, slow the economy, and ultimately hurt hard-working Americans. It is not responsible.

Opportunity is only half of America's basic bargain. The other half is responsibility.

2

Responsibility

IN THE AFTERMATH OF THE PLANE CRASH THAT
killed my friend, Secretary of Commerce Ron
Brown, and so many other fine Americans, I met
Ron's longtime friend and neighbor, Kent
Amos, at Ron's house. Let me tell you his story.

A decade and a half ago, Kent Amos was a successful executive in the Xerox Corporation and
the youngest director in its history. His wife, Carmen, also worked at Xerox. They live in Washington, D.C., where they raised their two
children, Wesley and Debbie. They also raised
eighty-seven other kids. The first ones were
friends of their own children—friends from bro-
ken homes, homes with a struggling single parent, or no home at all. They hung around the
Amos home after school, sometimes stayed on for
dinner and, after a while, stayed on to live. Many

of these kids were in trouble or on their way to it. The Amoses fed them, cared for them, made sure they studied hard every evening, attended and cheered at their games, and got most of them into college on scholarships. Each year the number grew. Kent and Carmen didn't save them all. They buried four of "their kids." Another one went to jail for burglary, joining his real father and stepfather in the same prison. But Kent made sure the boy got his GED while he was there and found work when his sentence was done.

The Amoses guess they've spent $20,000 or more of their own money every year raising these kids. Along the way, Kent created a non-profit organization that corporations like Xerox have helped support. Today his Urban Family Institute aims to reform the way families and communities nurture children so that no at-risk child grows up without the guidance, discipline, support, and love of a responsible, caring adult. He's found other families to help raise children and he's currently talking with Housing and Urban Development Secretary Henry Cisneros about turning public housing projects into "urban family universities" where parents and children can learn what they need to know to succeed in life.

Kent and Carmen Amos are a wonderful example of the American Dream at its best: They had opportunities that had been denied to earlier generations of African Americans, and they achieved success and prosperity. They exhibited responsibility in their individual, family, and work lives. But for them it wasn't enough. As Kent told me, he came to realize that if he wanted his children to have a positive, safe environment to learn and grow in, he had to extend his influence and his parenting to the classmates of his children. When he reached beyond his own children, Kent Amos began to build one of those remarkable villages it takes to raise our children as my wife Hillary said in her book on this subject.

I know we can't all invite a neighborhood full of troubled children into our homes and help raise them. But we can, each of us, be responsible first in our individual, family, and work lives, and then as citizens who do what they can to make our communities and nation strong.

Our Founders created a nation, as Lincoln said, "conceived in liberty." But they understood very clearly something many Americans forget: freedom works only when it is exercised with responsibility. For example, we have freedom of speech but also the responsibility to speak civilly, freedom of assembly but also the responsibility to assemble peaceably, freedom of the press but also the responsibility to be truthful, accurate, and fair.

Without responsibility, no free society can prosper. In the absence of responsibility, for example, free-market capitalism veers off into consumer fraud, insider trading, and abuse of employees. In the absence of responsibility, a mentality of entitlement creates narrow interest group politics, a rhetoric of helplessness, and an inability to serve the larger public interest. In the absence of responsibility, individual liberty is just selfishness. In each case, America's inherent community of purpose is weakened.

America is about more than individuals exercising their rights. Our brand of democracy is about individuals and families, business and labor, government and community organizations, all shouldering responsibility for our children, for our elders, for each other, and for generations yet to be born. Our Founding Fathers understood this. In the Preamble to our Constitution they said our objectives were not just to "secure the blessings of liberty to ourselves," but also "to our posterity." What's more, they said it was our job to "promote the general welfare." The former, they reasoned, would turn our attention away from immediate gratification and toward our responsibilities to our children. And the latter, they believed, would turn our attention away from ourselves and toward our responsibilities to each other. So from the beginning, opportunity and responsibility have gone hand in hand.

This political theory, though set out two centuries ago, is powerfully relevant today. When I was growing up, Americans could pretty much walk down the street of any city without fear of violent crime. Having children out of wedlock was rare and a source of shame. Not as many fathers walked away from their responsibilities to their children. Welfare was a way station for people who could work but were temporarily in a bind. In neighborhoods all across America, people could say what President Lyndon Johnson said when he left Washington to go back to his small hometown in Texas, "People know when you're sick and care when you die." For too many young people growing up today, that world exists only in black-and-white reruns on television.

People in public life are struggling to find solutions to these and other profound social problems. We all know that many of them are caused by a lack of personal responsibility: the teen mother who leaves school for a life on welfare; the deadbeat dad who walks away from his duty to his children; the criminal who preys upon the rest of us; the neighbors who turn their backs on the children in need; the business executive who fails to treat his employees right or who buries toxic wastes.

America was built upon a foundation of mutual responsibility. Strengthening that foundation is critical if we want our vision of the twenty-first century to become real. Since so many of the answers to our social problems require people to reassert control over their own lives and to assume responsibility for their conduct and their obligations, we have to develop community-based approaches that respond personally to these problems, not impersonally through large, out-dated bureaucracies. We must be willing to help people make decisions that are not destructive to them and costly for the rest of us. That is a national responsibility.

In the last four years, we have pursued this responsibility in four broad areas: first, strengthening individual and community responsibility through, among other things, welfare reform and crime prevention; second, meeting public responsibilities better by reinventing the federal government; third, encouraging businesses to take more responsibility for the welfare of their workers and their families; and fourth, working at all levels of society to address our responsibilities to future generations by improving how we protect our natural environment.

Government can help lead in each of these areas, but ultimately we must insist that citizens, businesses, and communities help themselves and assume responsibility for making the life of this great nation better person by person, family by family, block by block, community by community. The foundation, however, is individual responsibility. Before government responsibility, before corporate responsibility, before community responsibility, we must have individual responsibility.

Nowhere is the issue of individual responsibility better illustrated than welfare. For fifteen years— going back to my service as governor of Arkansas —I have worked to reform welfare, to make it a second chance not a way of life. I have talked with people on welfare, asked them what had happened to put them there and what it would take to turn their lives around. As a result of what I learned, Arkansas became a national leader in reforming a wide range of family and welfare programs. We lowered infant mortality by expanding maternal health services. We enhanced child care through a voucher system for working parents with modest incomes. We worked to reduce long-term welfare dependency by emphasizing education and train- ing, medical coverage, and child care, and then by requiring parents to take available work. We in- creased the involvement of even illiterate parents in the education of their preschool children. We increased child support enforcement before it be- came a national priority. And on behalf of the na- tion's governors, I helped write the 1988 federal welfare reform bill.

During the past three and a half years, we helped states create what *The New York Times* called "a quiet revolution on welfare." With little fanfare and no new legislation, we cut welfare red tape and approved welfare-to-work projects for some forty states and covering 75 percent of the people on welfare in this country. We imposed time limits, required work, required teen mothers to stay in school, and established much tougher enforcement of child-support orders, including enforcement across state lines.

And it has worked. There are 1.3 million fewer people on welfare today than there were when I took office. Food stamp rolls are down by more than 2 million. A few years ago, at a hearing, I asked a woman from Arkansas who had gotten off welfare what the best thing was about it. She looked me in the eye and said, "Now when my son goes to school and people ask him, 'What does your mother do for a living?' he can give an answer." You can't put a dollar figure on the pride behind that answer, or the positive impact it has on a child.

The look on that woman's face is one reason why I worked continuously with the Congress to try to reach agreement on legislation that would completely overhaul welfare nationally. I rejected two flawed bills Congress brought to my desk because they did not meet the basic test of responsible welfare reform: to be tough on work and responsibility, but not tough on children and parents who are responsible and want to work. Their willingness to keep working on a bill that would meet this test is why we have an historic overhaul of welfare today.

In 1991, I said we needed to end welfare as we know it. Now, with the passage of new welfare reform legislation, we have a chance to end a system that undermines the basic values of work, responsibility, and family that has trapped generation after generation in dependency and poverty, hurting the very people the system was designed to help.

In its place, we have an opportunity to establish a new system that meets the basic principles for reform I made clear from the beginning. First and foremost, it should be about moving people from welfare to work. Second, it should impose time limits of welfare benefits. Third, it should give people the child care and health care assistance they need to move from welfare to work without hurting their children.

The new law is rooted in these principles. It gives states and communities the chance to move people from dependence to independence and greater dignity. But, the real work is still to be done. States and communities have to make sure that jobs and child care are there. They can use money that used to go to welfare checks to pay for community service jobs or to give employers wage supplements for several months to encourage them to hire welfare recipients. They should also provide education and training when appropriate and must take care of those who, through no fault of their own, cannot find or do work. These are important, new responsibilities not just for welfare recipients, but for states, communities, and businesses. But if welfare reform is to work, all must shoulder their responsibilities.

I should also note that the welfare reform legislation is far from perfect, largely because of non-welfare provisions which contain excessive cuts designed to pay for excessive tax cuts in the Republican budget plan for high-income Americans who don't need them. There are parts of the legislation that are just plain wrong. We must work hard in the coming months and years to make them right. For example, the bill makes new cuts in child nutrition assistance that mostly hurt not welfare families, but our most hard-pressed working families who are already struggling to work themselves out of poverty. It also cuts off assistance to legal immigrants and their children. This is deeply unfair to legal immigrants who work hard and pay their taxes. The Republicans insisted on saying to those families, "You can work and pay taxes for three or four years, but if you or your children get into a car accident, develop a serious illness, or become a crime-victim, we won't help you." That is wrong, and we must make it right.

It is important to remember that this reform is just a beginning and that we must approach this historic moment with some humility. While we have learned much from the most successful state welfare reform initiatives, there is much we still do not know. We must implement this legislation in a way that truly moves people from welfare to work, and that is good for our children. We will be refining this reform for some time to come.

One thing we do know, however, is that just reforming welfare won't change the underlying social problems that have often led to welfare dependency. One of the most important of these problems is teenage pregnancy. Every year about a million teenagers become pregnant. In fact, nearly a third of all the babies born each year are to women under the age of eighteen, and not surprisingly, nearly 70 percent of these teens are unmarried. Teen pregnancy is not simply foolish and costly, it is destructive to children, to families, to our society. It is *wrong*. It is also an express ticket to poverty for the teenage mother. Nearly half of today's long-term welfare caseload are women who had their first child before the age of seventeen.

We cannot end the related cycles of welfare dependency and teen pregnancy unless we confront the issue of responsibility—the responsibility of young women not to get pregnant, the responsibility of men not to get them pregnant, the responsibility of fathers to support their children, the responsibility of parents to provide their children a safe home and teach them responsible sexual behavior and encourage abstinence, the responsibility of churches to support those teachings, the responsibility of community organizations to develop programs to help teen mothers and their children get a start in life, and the responsibility of public officials to understand that teen pregnancy is part of a complex web of social issues.

In the last three and a half years, we have done our part. I have challenged the states to require teen mothers to live at home or with a responsible adult. We now require teen mothers to stay in school and sign a personal responsibility contract to continue living at home—unless, of course, their home environment is abusive. For teens who can't go home, I have proposed seed money for "Second-Chance Homes," like those already established in several American communities, that provide safe and supportive community-organized and -operated residences for teen mothers and their children.

For the first time in years, teen pregnancy has leveled off and begun to drop. But this is a national problem and it needs national attention. That's why I challenged community, religious, and business leaders to shoulder more responsibility, and it is why I support the efforts of the National Campaign to Reduce Teen Pregnancy. To make sure that this issue is a top priority in the minds of our people, we are doing everything we can to spread the influence of community-based approaches that instill a sense of responsibility among our young people. And my administration is also funding abstinence-based programs to educate teenagers in our schools.

We need to tell children who have children: we care about you, but you have to care about yourself, too. Don't get pregnant or father a child until you are ready to shoulder that immense responsibility. If you do, we will help you only as long as you help yourself. And you can't walk away from that responsibility. If you do, we will make you assume it.

Our success on the child-support issue has demonstrated our resolve. In 1995, we collected a record $11 billion in child support, almost a 40 percent increase over 1992; since then I have directed states to require mothers to help identify and find absent fathers so we can make them support their children.

But we can and must do better. If all the people who owed child support paid it, 800,000 mothers and children would immediately leave the welfare rolls. The new welfare reform law gives us strong new tools to go after delinquent child support cases that cross state lines.

My message to deadbeat parents is simple: if you neglect your responsibilities, we will track you down, garnish your wages, suspend your licenses, and make you pay. It's not government's responsibility to support your children; it's yours.

Responsibility—individual and community—is also the key to America's crime problem. Only if we take greater responsibility for our own communities can we really achieve our objective of making the recent historic drop in the crime rate a long-term trend.

Ten days before the 1992 New Hampshire primary, I was in New York City to give a speech to a crowd gathered at a major hotel. As I made my way through the kitchen of the hotel, a worker in a hotel uniform came up and grabbed me. "Governor," he said in a thick immigrant's accent, "I want to talk to you." So I stopped and listened. "My ten-year-old boy," the man said, "he studies this election in school, and he has decided I should vote for you. But if I vote for you, I want you to do something for me.

"In the country where I come from," he went on, "we were very poor, but we were free. Here we have a park across the street from our apartment house, but my boy cannot play in it unless I am there with him, because he would be in danger. We have a school, a good school, only two blocks from our home, but my boy cannot walk to school unless I go with him.

"So if I vote for you," he said, looking me straight in the eye, "will you make my boy free?"

The most fundamental responsibility of any government is to protect the safety of its citizens. All of the other things government does on our behalf amount to very little if it fails in this task. If you can't walk down your street without looking over your shoulder, then this is not a free country and you are not a free person. We can't be as free as that hard-working immigrant's child—and every child—deserves to be, unless crime is brought under control.

I took office determined to take a new approach to fighting crime. Let's remember what things were like then. Violent crime had been rising for four straight years. Convicted felons could walk into any gun shop and buy a handgun. Assault weapons with no purpose other than to kill people were sold as freely as hunting rifles and shotguns. Ordinary, law-abiding Americans were afraid to walk the streets of their own neighborhoods, even afraid of sending their children to school. Blocked by the gun lobby's allies in Congress, efforts to bring some sanity to the situation had been stalled for years.

I was determined to change all this. Determined to punish criminals, not make excuses for their behavior. Determined to keep guns out of the wrong hands. Determined to prevent crime before it happens by, among other things, giving young people something to say yes to. And above all, determined to restore the role of police at the center of every neighborhood in America.

Much of law enforcement is a local and state responsibility, but the federal government can help, and I was determined to find the resources to provide that help. That's what my 1994 Crime Bill did.

But I also knew that the federal government alone couldn't solve the crime problem; ultimately it has to be solved on the streets of American neighborhoods every day, by individuals acting responsibly and by communities working together to enforce responsible behavior.

That's what we have been doing, and we are making progress. In 1995, for the fourth year in a row, the rate of serious crimes dropped. Murder dropped 8 percent, robberies 7 percent, rape 6 percent and burglary 5 percent. New York City has had the biggest crime drop since 1972. Houston, one of the leaders in the community policing movement, has the lowest murder rate it has had in nineteen years.

Because we will never eliminate the darkness that lurks in human nature, there will never be a time when there is no crime, no violence in America. But we can make it the exception, not the rule. My goal is to create an America where when people turn on the evening news and the lead story is a serious crime, they are surprised and shocked, instead of just accepting it as news as usual and inevitable.

To reach that goal, I believe we needed a new approach—one that combined all the tools available to us: *police, punishment,* and *prevention.* And to wield these tools, we need not just the government, not just the criminal justice system, but every American in every community in the nation to take responsibility for winning back our streets and our children's future.

My 1994 Crime Bill is fulfilling a commitment I made to the American people to put 100,000 new police officers on the street to strengthen community policing. It's an old idea, really. It means getting police out of the police station, out of the squad cars, and back on the street, back in the neighborhood where they can work with neighbors to spot criminals, shut down crack houses, prevent domestic violence, get to know children on the block, and stop crime before it happens.

Community policing works not just because more officers are on the streets, but because neighbors get involved. The federal government can put 100,000 new officers in police departments around the country, but if we don't have citizens in neighborhoods, schools, and businesses who are prepared to support those police, if we don't have parents who will shoulder their responsibility to teach kids right from wrong, then we won't succeed. When police are walking down the street, they ought to feel like every law-abiding citizen is walking with them. Neighbors helping neighbors, friends sticking up for friends, parents teaching children the difference between right and wrong, residents establishing bonds of trust with police officers—that's what community policing is all about.

Fighting crime is every American's responsibility. It's not just a public issue; it's a personal matter. It's picking up a phone and calling for help when you see somebody in trouble. It's been more than thirty years since Kitty Genovese was left to die on a street in New York City by neighbors who closed their windows and drew their shades when they heard her screams. We cannot let that era return. That's why I have called on 1 million Americans to volunteer to participate in neighborhood watch activities in their communities helping our police to keep our streets and our neighborhoods safe. And that's why I asked the cellular phone industry to provide free airtime and 50,000 cellular phones to those neighborhood watch groups across the country. The industry has responded with enthusiasm and generosity, and I hope the American people will answer the challenge as well.

We each have responsibilities and there are almost unlimited opportunities by which we can meet them. We can join a neighborhood watch group or help form one. We can spend a few hours a week helping young people in a boys' or girls' club or a D.A.R.E. anti-drug program. That's how crime gets fought: citizen by citizen, block by block, neighborhood by neighborhood.

Good policing, however, needs to be matched with tough punishment. Our Crime Bill and, more recently, our Anti-Terrorism Bill, did just that. We have pushed states to adopt the rule the government uses on federal prisoners that requires them to serve 85 percent of their sentence, without parole. For those who commit violent crimes repeatedly, we have made "three strikes and you're out" the law of the land. We expanded the application of the death penalty for nearly sixty violent crimes, including murder of a federal law enforcement officer, and limited excessive death row appeals. And we have stiffened sentences for drug offenders and told those involved in drug activities in public housing projects they only get one strike. Public housing is a privilege; abuse it and you're out.

We've also cracked down on men who stalk, threaten, or abuse women and children by establishing tough new penalties to enforce protection orders, by connecting domestic abuse files to the system we use for firearm background checks, and by establishing a national Domestic Violence Hotline. Through that Hotline (1-800-799-SAFE), some 7,000 women a month who are in trouble now are able to get help quickly, find shelter, and report abuse to authorities.

Though tough punishment is important, every police officer will tell you we can't jail our way out of our crime problem; we must do more to prevent crime before it happens. Today, after years of fighting special interests, America finally has the Brady Bill, a commonsense law that establishes a five-day waiting period and a background check that has already kept handguns out of the hands of some 60,000 felons, fugitives, and other criminals.

We also have a law that bans the sale of nineteen assault weapons—guns made expressly for killing people. What's more, not a single hunter in America has lost a weapon or missed a season as a result of either the assault weapons ban or the Brady Bill. Furthermore, we have new tools to fight terrorism at home and abroad, and a new National Drug Control Strategy that targets young people for education and prevention, pulls drug users off the streets and puts them in treatment, aims to reduce the cost of drug abuse to our health and welfare systems, and seeks to block drugs at the border and cut off drugs at their source.

Prevention is the strategy that holds the best hope—indeed, the only real hope—for breaking the crime cycle. If you don't believe it, ask the police officers on the beat in any city in America. They will tell you that stopping drugs, stopping gangs, stopping handguns and assault weapons, and stopping the conditions that breed criminal behavior are what stops crime.

The combination of police, punishment, and prevention has brought the crime rate down. But we have much more work to do and many of the very initiatives that have produced these improvements are at risk. Funding has been made available so far for about 44,000 of the 100,000 new police officers we need for community policing; we're ahead of schedule but the congressional Republicans have tried repeatedly to repeal the law. The gun lobby and its allies in Congress are working hard to repeal the assault weapons ban and prevent measures to make it easier to track the origin of explosives or ban cop-killer bullets. Most, but not all, congressional Republicans continue to reject prevention programs, preferring more jails to incarcerate criminals after they commit crimes, instead of community efforts to stop crime before it happens. We must fight to preserve these reforms, fully implement them, and keep reducing crime. And we should have a constitutional amendment to give crime victims the right to be involved, and to be informed about and make statements at court proceedings such as bail setting, plea bargaining, sentencing, and parole.

Finally, there is one looming crime issue that is of deep and growing concern to parents, and indeed all Americans, an issue we are only beginning to bring under control. It is the issue of youth crime—or more accurately, the twin issues of crimes committed by youths and crimes committed against youths. Murders of teenagers rose 82 percent from 1984 to 1994. Gun violence is now the second leading cause of death among young people between the ages of ten and nineteen. Much of this violence is by young people against young people. It often arises out of alcohol or drug abuse or drug dealing, and often it is organized—by gangs.

A big part of the problem is that so many young people entering their teens are children who were born out of wedlock, have grown up without the guidance of both parents, have lived in difficult and even dangerous family situations, and have been out there essentially raising themselves. Many of these children turn their lives around, but many others don't, slipping into a shadowy world of crime, drugs, gangs, and violence.

All Americans should care about these children. Their futures will be ours. And even if we can't do what Kent and Carmen Amos are doing, we have to be willing to do our part to build the village it will take to raise them into successful adults, to teach them right from wrong, to give them a future to look forward to, to pass on the character and values they need to reach that future. A lot of Americans are already doing so.

At the same time, we need to protect ourselves and our children from violent youthful offenders. Since I took office, we've made it a federal crime for any person under the age of eighteen to carry a handgun unless supervised by an adult, and have required schools to expel for one year any student who brings a gun to school. We've encouraged schools to get tough on school violence and to adopt uniform policies like the one they have in Long Beach, California, to help re-

duce violence while promoting dignity and respect. We've endorsed curfew policies like the
one they have in New Orleans, which reduces
children's exposure to danger. We've supported
one of the most effective steps we can take,
which is also one of the most old-fashioned:
making sure we enforce truancy laws so that our
children are learning in the classroom and not
on our streets. And I supported and signed
"Megan's Law," named after seven-year-old
Megan Kanka, who was raped and murdered
two years ago by a twice-convicted child moles-
ter who lived on her block. The new law requires states to notify communities of released or
paroled child molesters and sex offenders.

Finally, we have established a National Gang
Tracking Network and sent a clear message to
the gangs that are at the root of today's drug cul-
ture and youth violence: we mean to put you out
of business, to break the backs of your organizations, to stop you from terrorizing our neighborhoods and our children, and to put you away for
a very long time.

But we still have work to do. This year I submitted legislation to further toughen treatment of

violent youth offenders, and a few months ago I announced the creation of a new computer system to reverse the rise in gun violence by tracking guns to their source. In Boston, a pilot version of this initiative has been so successful that no juveniles have been killed by handguns so far this year. All our efforts are designed to rescue kids in trouble. At night children belong at home, under a curfew, if necessary. During the day they belong in school, not on the street. At any time, our children are *our* responsibility.

Cutting crime off at its roots is a task that belongs to every citizen in America. This summer we got some good news. The violent crime arrest rate for juveniles dropped for the first time in seven years. And the juvenile murder arrest rate dropped by 15 percent, the largest one-year decrease in more than a decade. But the problem is still profound. It will take all our efforts, community by community, to keep our teenagers away from drugs and violence.

In dealing with our welfare and crime problems it's clear that the federal government alone cannot begin to provide the solutions. Responsibility must be borne more broadly by all regions of our national community—business, labor, religious, community, and local government groups. Still, the federal government can play an important role in meeting these challenges, as this chapter illustrates.

Exactly what the federal government should do, and how it should do it, are especially critical questions as we deal with the dramatic changes in work and family life and the other new challenges of the twenty-first century. That's why rethinking and reinventing government has been a priority in the last several years.

The Founders created the federal government to do what only a national government could do. It started with the basics that remain critical today: national defense, foreign affairs, our financial system, and, of course, the protection of our constitutional rights and enforcement of federal laws. It grew to include protection and management of our national lands, agriculture, and commerce. Then it encompassed an increasingly broad range of social concerns as the problems and the successes of our Industrial Age mounted. Later, the Cold War and America's social and economic challenges led both Republican and

Democratic administrations to work to limit abuse in the workplace and the market system, to protect those in need, advance the course of education and the environment, deal with atomic energy, expand civil rights, and more. We have been expanding our vision of a "united states" ever since the failure of the Articles of Confederation caused the states to agree on a national Constitution, with a federal government to help achieve important public purposes that could not be achieved by citizens, the free-market system, or state and local governments acting on their own.

That is how government grew—with the consent of the governed. But America has always been skeptical of "big government." As has often been noted, during most of our history, we have remained philosophically conservative about the role of government even when we have favored specific activist measures because the problems of the time required them.

Our age-old debate about the role of the federal government has acquired a new energy and urgency in our time for these reasons: first, none of the old approaches to our social problems seem to have worked very well; second, in a world of intense global competition, we can't afford a government that is wasteful and too bureaucratic; and third, the revolution in information technology, and the organization of work, makes it important that government learn to do more with less, to be more entrepreneurial and more effective.

Has our government grown too big? In significant ways, yes. Many of today's operations still run like monopolistic, big industrial corporations, with top-down, command-and-control management, lots of micro-management through rules and regulations, and a mass-production, one-size-fits-all approach to both service and regulation. That model doesn't work in industry anymore; that's why there has been such an intense effort in the private sector to increase productivity and flexibility. Government, however, was slow to recognize this and even slower to respond.

The question now is, how should we change government? Ever since the Reagan Revolution of 1980, the dominant Republican argument has shifted from "less government is almost always better than more of it" to "government is always the problem." That argument reached its peak in this Congress' budget and its legislative initiatives that would have crippled our environmental and public-health efforts.

Our administration and the new Democratic party take a different view. We say the era of big government is over, but we must not go back to an era of "every man for himself." We need government to do those things which are essential to giving us the tools we need to make the most of our own lives, to honoring our obligations to one another, to building a strong economy, to protecting the public health and our environment. We believe we can shrink the size of government, reduce its burden, and improve its ability to help Americans meet the challenges of the new era and protect our values. There is simply no evidence that America can be better off if we abandon our attempt to go forward together and leave America's future to the tender mercies of the global marketplace.

The truth is, Americans don't want our government gutted. We know from experience that there are some things that government must or should do: protect us against enemies, foreign and domestic, come to our aid when disaster strikes, help fight crime, ensure the health and well-being of the weakest among us, restore and preserve our environment, ensure the safety of our food, provide for the needs of those who have defended our country in uniform, provide everyone with access to quality education. The main reason I rejected Congress's budget bill last year was because it abandoned many of these responsibilities, especially those involving education, the environment, and the care of children and the elderly.

We don't want our government in our face, but we do want it on our side when we need it, and quickly. We don't want, for example, a weak Federal Emergency Management Agency when there's an earthquake, a flood, or a horrible tragedy like Oklahoma City. We don't want a gutted Occupational Health and Safety Administration when the place where we work is unsafe. We don't want a Food and Drug Administration that can't guarantee that the food we feed our children won't harm them.

The real issue isn't big government versus small government.

I believe America needs a government that is both smaller and more responsive. One that both works better and costs less. One that shifts authority from the federal level to states and locali-

ties as much as possible. One that relies upon en-
trepreneurs in the private sector when the private
sector can do the job best. One that has fewer
regulations and more incentives. One, in short,
that has more common sense and seeks more
common ground.

And now that's what America is getting.
Under the Reinventing Government initiative
led by Vice President Gore, we have reduced the
federal workforce by over 225,000 workers, are
dumping 16,000 pages of burdensome and often
outdated regulations, and have cut nearly 200
programs and projects. We've also brought about
political reforms—such as passing the line item
veto, ending unfunded federal mandates, requiring Congress to abide by the same laws as the rest
of the country, reforming our lobbying laws to
limit abuse, and passing the motor voter law—
that will, I believe, increase public confidence in
our government.

We haven't stopped at cutting; we have changed
and improved the government that remains. Here
are a few examples. We've made service agencies
more customer friendly. Last year, *Business Week*
magazine rated the Social Security Administration
the number one provider of telephone service to

customers, ahead of great companies like L.L. Bean and Federal Express. The enforcement arms of the Occupational Safety and Health Administration and the Environmental Protection Agency are creating new regulatory partnerships with incentives to advance the public interest so they can act less like regulatory cops. The Food and Drug Administration, without abdicating its duty to protect the health of the American people, has reduced dramatically the approval time for badly needed drugs, including those which have helped to increase the length and quality of life for people with HIV and AIDS. The Federal Communications Commission, which used to license spectrum for wireless services for free, has auctioned large segments of spectrum to the private sector, bringing billions of dollars into our Treasury, helping to bring the deficit down. The Federal Emergency Management Agency, which a few years ago was an emergency itself, is now so responsive to those in need that they're receiving accolades from everyone they serve. The Small Business Administration has reduced its loan application form from an inch-thick to a single page, speeded approval times, and doubled its loan volume since 1992, including a huge increase in loans to qualified women and minority businesses even as its loss rate has declined—all with a smaller budget. The Department of Housing and Urban Development has formed a partnership with the private sector to spur home ownership to record levels; it is giving more poor people vouchers to select their own housing, and is now committed to destroying some 30,000 units of bad, crime-ridden public housing around the country and replacing them with new, safer, cleaner garden apartment complexes where new rules promote self-sufficiency and responsibility. HUD and the FHA have also cut the average closing costs for first-time homebuyers by $1,000. The Agriculture Department has modernized and strengthened meat and poultry safety regulations for the first time in twenty years. The Education Department has cut the cost of student loans, reduced the default rate, and given students the option of paying loans back as a percentage of their income. The list is long, and getting longer every year as our Reinventing Government initiative continues to gain momentum.

Reinvention works. It doesn't just shrink the federal government, it changes it. It takes us beyond the stale old debate between more government or less government to a government that is smaller *and* better. In so doing, it helps restore America's government to its rightful owners, the American people.

The federal government has another critical responsibility: creating the framework in which our economy can grow. By reducing the deficit, bringing interest rates down, holding inflation in check, restraining bad business practices, expanding opportunities for world trade, supporting research and technology, and increasing educational opportunity, the government plays a central role.

Government, however, doesn't create jobs; that's businesses' responsibility, and American businesses have been meeting that responsibility brilliantly. Of the more than 10 million new jobs created since I became President, 93 percent of them have been in the private sector.

But creating jobs isn't businesses' only responsibility in American society. American business, the engine of our prosperity and the envy of the world, has clear responsibilities if we want people to have better lives, provide for their families, and face the future with confidence. Let me be clear: the most fundamental responsibility for any business is to make a profit, to create jobs and income by competing and growing. But one of the implications of the downsizing of the federal government is that businesses today have more responsibility not only to grow and do well, but to help in dealing with the dislocations and challenges this new era imposes on American workers, their families, and their communities.

I recognize that not every business can afford to do more than worry about its bottom line, especially a lot of small businesses. But many of America's most successful businesses have struck a new bargain with their employees: employees work to make the company more profitable, and the company works to make employees more valuable. Put another way, they're treating employees not as raw materials, but as the indispensable assets they are.

Consider NUCOR, a steelmaker that just doesn't believe in layoffs. NUCOR's workers are paid a fairly modest base salary, but they get a weekly bonus based on the company's performance. When the company does well, the workers share fairly in the success. If there is a downturn, no one is laid off. Instead, the sacrifice is equally shared. Executive pay is tied to the company's performance just like worker pay. Last year, the average NUCOR steelworker earned over $50,000. And every worker with a college-age child gets up to $2,200 tuition allowance. Or consider Harman International, the stereo speaker company. To avoid laying off their employees when business got slow—employees in whom they've invested a lot—Harman went into a business with its employees and created Off Line Enterprises, in which workers can use Harman's scrap materials to produce entirely new products of their own. It keeps the employees working and creative, it makes the company money, and it tells every employee the company cares about them and values them. Or consider Procter & Gamble, which believes in families so much it gives up to a year of maternity leave, reduces work hours for new parents for up to five years, and subsidizes child care.

Major corporations aren't the only ones shouldering these responsibilities. There are companies like Fel-Pro, Incorporated, a four-generation family-owned company that makes auto supplies and provides its employees, 50 percent of whom are minorities, with everything from personal legal and family counseling services to a full-time wellness center, from a summer camp for employees' kids to tuition for further training. Fel-Pro's Kenneth Lehman said at the Corporate Citizenship Conference I hosted this year, "Conventional thinking places extensive family-friendly benefits and corporate profits at opposite ends of the spectrum. However, we feel our benefits enhance our profits, and as long as our bottom line confirms this, we'll keep doing it."

These companies don't make the headlines, but they're doing well by doing good. They're creating family-friendly workplaces, providing health coverage, pensions, and training, forming new partnerships with workers, and providing safe workplaces. They're strengthening their bottom line *and* investing in the well-being of their employees. The result for their employees? More choices, and as a result, greater overall security for themselves and their families. The result for the businesses? Lower turnover, higher loyalty, better, more flexible employees. It's a good bargain, one not unlike America's basic bargain: the marrying of opportunity with responsibility. Another of the CEOs who attended the Corporate Citizenship Conference this year believes a corporation's responsibilities extend even beyond the well-being of its employees to the well-being of the planet. Yvon Chouinard, the founder of Patagonia, the outdoor clothing and equipment company, told me that in addition to doing daily environmental assessments to minimize the extent to which his company pollutes, Patagonia contributes one percent of its sales to safeguard and restore the environment. According to Chouinard, "Our customers appreciate our efforts and all of us feel a little less helpless in trying to leave a habitable earth for our children."

Safeguarding the environment is one national, even global obligation for which we are all responsible. Four years ago, on the twenty-second anniversary of Earth Day, I said that America needed to make a new covenant for the environment, one that commits us to leave our children a nation whose air, water, and land are unspoiled, whose natural beauty is undimmed, whose leadership for sustainable growth is unsurpassed. I also said that to achieve those goals, we had to make environmental protection and enhancement a common task—one to which every citizen, every community, every business and corporation, and every level of government is committed. And while the task before us is great, that is exactly what's happening.

Here's just one unusual example. In New York City, in the heart of the ravaged South Bronx, a cancer had eaten away at the soul of a neighborhood struggling to survive. For a quarter of a century, the nineteen-acre abandoned switchyard of the old Harlem Rail Yard of the New York Central Railroad festered, its soil steeped in pollution, its bleak expanse covered with trash and debris. In time it became a mecca for drug dealers, gangsters, and criminals of all kinds.

Today, however, one of the most disadvantaged neighborhoods in the nation is being reborn, and its heart is . . . that same old Harlem Rail Yard.

A local community development corporation, a national environmental organization, and two international paper companies have joined together to build a state-of-the-art paper plant on the site. Maya Lin, the architect who created the Vietnam Memorial in Washington, D.C., is designing the plant. With the most advanced production, energy efficiency, and pollution control technologies, the Bronx Community Paper Company, which will create several hundred permanent jobs, is the largest manufacturing plant built in the city since the Second World War.

What's more, no trees will be cut for this plant to produce paper. Instead, the half-billion-dollar plant will harvest New York City's "urban forest"—the tons of used paper generated in the city's office buildings every day—to produce 100 percent recycled newsprint. It will also use reclaimed water from a sewage treatment plant for 80 percent of its water needs.

And that's not all. It will help fund a dormitory for up to twenty students attending the local high school who do not have stable homes; a South Bronx Family Learning Center to provide residents with health care, child care, literacy classes, employment and training assistance, and housing opportunities; a new retail center; upgrading at local libraries; a working capital revolving loan fund for housing and business development; and a children's endowment fund to expand educational opportunities for the neighborhood's kids. How did it happen? The government's role was limited and market oriented. Not long ago, I signed an executive order requiring all federal agencies to use recycled paper. That action alone created a huge new market for recycled paper producers nationwide. But the real credit goes to the community and corporate officials who worked hard over four years to bring the project to life.

The old Harlem Rail Yard in the Bronx is no Yellowstone. It's no Everglades. It's not the Alaskan wilderness or the California desert. But it illustrates an important environmental lesson nonetheless. Over the years, America's abundance of land and resources fostered a "disposable" mentality in which we took what we needed and threw away what we didn't. Now that ethic has come back to haunt us. There are thousands of toxic waste sites in neighborhoods throughout the country. There are thousands of acres of used-up and abandoned land. There are timber-stripped hillsides, overgrazed rangelands, threatened wildlife habitats, and unsafe water supplies. What the Bronx Community Paper Company teaches us is that we have the power, if we muster the will, to reverse these conditions. With creativity and cooperation, we can recover lost pieces of America's environment, return them to good health, protect other lands and resources from being destroyed, and even create environmentally friendly jobs in the process.

And that's what we're doing. In only twenty-five years we have cut toxic emissions from factories in half. Lead levels in children's blood are down 70 percent. Thousands of miles of streams and rivers, once so polluted that one caught fire, are clean. Lake Erie, once pronounced dead, now teems with fish. Many endangered species, from the most humble to the most exalted, the American bald eagle, are recovering. Wild lands, scenic rivers, wildlife refuges, once threatened, are now protected.

But much remains to be done. A third of us still breathes air that endangers our health. Our national parks are badly in need of funds for adequate maintenance and staffing. Many species remain in danger of extinction. In too many communities the water is unsafe to drink. Some 10 million children under twelve live and play within four miles of a toxic waste dump. We have cleaned up a lot of our waterways, but more than a third of our streams still need work.

The list of work to be done is long, but we have made considerable progress. In the last four years, we've expanded the community right-to-know law, which requires industries to tell our citizens what substances are released into our air and water. We're cutting toxic air pollution from chemical plants by 90 percent. Because of tougher clean-air laws, 50 million Americans in fifty-five cities are now breathing easier. Working closely with both consumer groups and the meat- and poultry-processing industries, we've overhauled the inspection system—for the first time in nearly a century—so that scientific tests are now used to assure that when parents serve their children a chicken dinner or take them out for a hamburger, they can be confident the food is safe. Working with some of our country's best corporate citizens, we kicked dozens of dangerous chemicals out of the marketplace and quickly replaced them with safer substitutes.

How we protect the environment is also important. In the early days, environmental protection was too often a battleground between opposing sides determined to fight for their extreme positions: either more regulation or no regulation. Unwilling to negotiate, they almost always fought to a stalemate and their battles ended up in court; court-established solutions often left little room for common sense and produced deep resentment and enduring suspicion. The whole process polarized and divided many Americans over one of those rare things that truly does bring us together as a people: our natural environment.

I have never believed we had to choose between either a clean and safe environment or a growing economy. Protecting the health and safety of all Americans doesn't have to come at the expense of our economy's bottom line. And creating thriving companies and new jobs doesn't have to come at the expense of the air we breathe, the water we drink, the food we eat, or the natural landscape in which we live. We can, and indeed must, have both.

That's why, during my administration, we've changed the government's approach to safeguarding the environment. Today we're creating more partnerships between environmentalists and people working in the private sector. I believe in focusing on results, not just on rulemaking. And I believe in flexibility in achieving those results. In the last three and a half years, we've taken steps to cut 15 million hours of paperwork at the Environmental Protection Agency. We've lifted 27,000 so-called Brownfield urban sites from the Superfund inventory that need no further action, and made them available again for much-needed industrial and commercial development, and we've shielded some 12,000 small firms from liability at Superfund sites where their involvement was minimal. We are encouraging responsible companies to create their own inexpensive, efficient ways of exceeding pollution standards and then, when they do, throwing away the rule book. Through our Common Sense Initiative government officials, environmentalists, and industry leaders are working together to create environmental protection strategies that are cleaner, cheaper, and smarter to protect the health of all Americans and the natural resources we share.

We're taking the same approach in managing the public's natural resources. We're sitting down with landowners in vital wildlife habitats around the country to draw up Habitat Management Plans that protect rare species before they become endangered and protect the landowners from future government constraints. We are using similar techniques for timber, rangeland, and national parks management.

But despite this sea change in environmental protection, there is trouble ahead. For twenty-five years, cleaning up the environment has been a bipartisan effort. But now that's changing. For the first time, the gains America has made in cleaning up the environment and in maintaining good stewardship of our natural resources are at risk. Last year a small army of lobbyists for polluters descended on Capitol Hill and mounted a full-scale assault on the environment and on public health. They sat down with their allies in the Congress to rewrite environmental laws and weaken the safeguards people of good faith from both parties worked for a generation to create. They knew the American people would never put up with the outright repeal of our environmental laws, so they took the stealth approach: they proposed a budget that made it impossible to enforce the laws of the land and, at the same time, quietly began submitting bills and special-interest riders that would gut one environmental protection after another.

They proposed closing or selling off some of our national parks and have cut funding for maintenance. They proposed shifting the burden of paying for toxic waste cleanup from the polluters themselves to the taxpayer, while at the same time cutting the Superfund budget by 25 percent. They proposed loopholes in the Clean Air Act to benefit polluting industries and have cut the funds for setting clean air standards. They proposed cutting funding for safe drinking water by 45 percent and for water infrastructure—pipes, pumps, treatment plants—by 29 percent. They tried to remove protections from millions of acres of wilderness, including the Alaska National Wildlife Refuge.

They tried to expand taxpayer-supported clear-cutting of the Tongass National Forest in Alaska. They proposed giving away mining and grazing rights on public lands at a tiny fraction of their true market value. They tried to create a new multibillion dollar entitlement program that would require taxpayers to pay polluters not to pollute. They tried, in essence, to repeal the Clean Water Act and Endangered Species Act. Perhaps most insidious of all, they proposed rolling back the law that gives people a right to know what pollutants companies are releasing into their neighborhoods.

I have vetoed every attack on the environment that has come across my desk and will continue to do so until those in Congress who propose them realize that the heart of the word "conservative" is "conserve."

And as we move forward, there is still much we need to do to make new progress—in restoring the Everglades, rebuilding facilities at our national parks, seeking a binding international agreement to reduce the kind of air pollution that leads to global warming, and eliminating all toxic waste dumps from one end of this country to the other. And I look forward to setting as a national goal the extension of our efforts to enhance water quality, to clean up toxic chemicals, and to extend the right-to-know to communities and neighborhoods across America.

There are some encouraging signs on the horizon. Stung by public outrage, Congress has moderated its assault on environmental and public health protection and just before the August recess adopted, virtually unanimously, two very important bills: the Safe Drinking Water Act and a law to protect us from pesticides in our food. I applaud those Republicans who have returned to supporting the environment, and the Democrats who protected it under withering attack.

For a quarter of a century, Americans have stood as one to say no to dirty air, toxic food, and poisoned water, and to say yes to leaving this land to our children as unspoiled as their hopes. I have no intention of letting special interests subvert this long-standing national interest.

The environment is not a luxury, it is our home. It is not an option, it is the air we breathe, the water we drink, the life we live. Environmental preservation is about self-preservation and about the preservation of our children's future. Maintaining and enhancing our environment, passing on a clean planet to future generations, is a sacred obligation of citizenship and perhaps our ultimate responsibility. Our environment is, quite literally, our common ground. And preserving it for future generations deepens the sense of community we must have to build a strong future together.

For all Americans, responsibility is simply the flip side of opportunity, and together they represent the two sides of the coin of citizenship in this great nation. When opportunity and responsibility are in balance, when each is given equal value—in our families, our businesses, our neighborhoods, and the nation as a whole— we achieve the objective we all seek, a community of purpose and a clearer vision of the American Dream—a dream we all hope to share as part of our American community.

3

Community

E ARLIER THIS YEAR, I WAS IN WASHINGTON STATE to inspect the damage from the devastating floods they had there, and I stopped in the little community of Woodland to visit with some folks working on the cleanup effort. I met a man in his mid-sixties who was retired from the local utility company, a naturalized immigrant from Norway. That man had been operating a jackhammer for eight hours—with a cracked rib—doing what he could to help his neighbors rebuild. Nearby, I spent some time with a couple in their seventies who had lost nearly everything but had somehow retained their sense of humor. The husband said to me, "You know, before today we wouldn't have been fit to welcome a President. But come on in and look; today I can offer you an indoor swimming pool!" We all had a good laugh, and then he turned to me and said, "You know, as awful as this is, people have come in here to help us and they've been here every day since the flood happened. Don't you just wish we could behave this way all the time?"

Perhaps the most sweeping lesson I have learned in the last three and a half years is this: when we are divided, we defeat ourselves; when we work together as a community, America always wins. In an era when the decibel level of partisan shouting often drowns out the quiet toiling of those who work to achieve real progress, it's easy to lose track of the fact that working together to achieve common ground is one of our most important national values. It is our constant challenge to protect it against the forces that seek to divide us.

That spirit of common purpose was in full evidence, for example, after the tragedy of Oklahoma City: the courage and tireless work of doctors, nurses, paramedics, and rescuers from all over the country; the resilience and grit of the people who set to work rebuilding right from the very first day; the determination and personal bravery of those who were injured or lost loved ones; and the compassionate donations from Americans everywhere to those in need. Working together is what Americans do best. We rise to the occasion and pitch in, whether it's floods in the Midwest or wounded children in Bosnia.

A hundred and fifty years ago, the great nineteenth-century French commentator on America, Alexis de Tocqueville, marveled at our eagerness to form associations and called it perhaps our most distinctive characteristic as a nation. Yet there are so many loud voices that seek to divide us for political or commercial purposes. And when we see black churches burned, or synagogues and Islamic centers desecrated, or swastikas painted on the doors of African American Special Forces members at Fort Bragg, we know we are not immune to the kinds of evil forces that, left unrestrained, have brought such heartache and ruin to so many all over the world.

The distinguished political scientist Robert Putnam has researched what it takes for nations and communities to succeed and concluded it comes down to three things: rules, networks, and trust. And trust comes when people relate to each other across the lines that divide them as members of community groups, what Putnam calls "networks." In his study, "Bowling Alone," Putnam found troubling trends that suggested a deterioration of the networks of common interest that have been critical to our success since Tocqueville and before. I had the same feeling in 1991. I wanted to help reinspire a sense of common purpose, to help rebuild those citizen networks, and the trust which any great nation must have to thrive. That was one of the most important reasons I sought the presidency.

But I believe our sense of community is growing again. Indeed, wherever I go in this country, I see Americans joining groups, working together, seeking common ground, searching out joint solutions to make this a better country. Look around our communities. We see people working together toward common purposes everywhere: in efforts to strengthen schools, in neighborhood revitalization programs, in block watches, in campaigns to create performing arts centers, and in a thousand other ways every day. Especially when it comes to taking more community responsibility for saving our children from violence, gangs, and drugs, for helping our families to be strong, and reinforcing the sense of our fundamental values, there is a growing tide of effective community action all across America.

Take a penny from your pocket. On one side, next to Lincoln's portrait, is a single word: "Liberty." On the other side is our national motto. It says *E Pluribus Unum*—"Out of Many, One." It does not say "Every Man for Himself."

That humble penny is an explicit declaration— one you can carry around in your pocket—that America is about *both* individual liberty and community obligation. These two commitments—to protect personal freedom and seek common ground—are the coin of our realm, the measure of our worth.

Historically, there was a practical as well as a moral reason for emphasizing civic responsibility when it came time to write our Declaration of Independence in 1776. When the Founders declared that governments are "instituted among men, deriving their just powers from the consent of the governed," they were making two radical assertions. The first was that government could be a servant of the people, rather than the other way around—a commitment we would all do well to remember more often. The second was that free people, to remain free, must work together to forge consent—they must balance their private interests with the public interest, their own welfare with the general welfare of the community and the nation.

In short, America is not just about independence, but also about *interdependence.* And it was to both that our Founders in the Declaration of Independence said they would "mutually pledge our lives, our fortunes and our sacred honor."

The lesson of America's history is that the good life is about more than individual liberty and material well-being; it's about cultivating community relationships and attending to public concerns.

Hope and Hot Springs, Arkansas, the towns where I grew up, were what we used to call tight-knit communities. That's a very revealing phrase. It meant the fabric of community life was strong and whole. You not only knew your neighbors, you looked out for them and your neighbors looked out for you. You not only worked with your neighbors during the week, but you worked together with them on community projects on the weekend. In those towns, and in other towns and city neighborhoods across America, we had a "community of purpose." And that's still what we want. Americans want to be part of a nation that's coming together, not coming apart. We want to be part of a community where people look out for each other, not just for themselves.

We live in and have responsibilities to many communities at once. First, our families are perhaps the smallest and most important community in which we live, and meeting our obligations to them has grown steadily more difficult as competing pressures, especially the pressures of earning a living, have increased. Second, we live in neighborhoods and communities that are increasingly diverse and require the faith, hard work, and good will of all of us if we are to sustain our nation as a font of liberty and opportunity. And third, we live in a community of nations, a global village in which we have both good and bad neighbors, all of whom we must deal with every day.

Our ability to build strong communities begins
with building strong families. We know that if
the first few years of a child's life go right, with
involved, caring parents to love and encourage
them, teach them right from wrong and set an
example, it can make the difference between a
lifetime of hope and fulfillment or one of despair
and disappointment. It can also mean the difference between an America prepared to meet the
challenges of the twenty-first century, with its
core values protected, and one that is not. To
paraphrase Walt Whitman, "Produce good children; the rest follows."

But these days, that's not so easy to do. A host
of problems besets even the most vigilant parents
and the best children: television and music that
seem to condone violence and inappropriate sexual activity, along with negative peer pressure,
manifested in its most extreme form by gangs in
disadvantaged neighborhoods, to name a few. In
some families, poverty, abusive or simply absent
parents, alcoholism, and drug addiction jeopar-
dize kids' chances.

In most families, just the pressures of modern life itself are making it hard to give children the time, energy, and attention they need. With parents working full-time jobs, maybe even going to classes on the side, and shuttling kids to the organized activities they need because they can't just play in the streets like we used to, raising a family is hard, hard work.

In fact, for most families, it's harder to succeed both at home and at work these days. Yet any society that forces people to make a choice between these two things is going to fail. If Americans can only succeed at work by failing at home, we're in trouble. And if they can only succeed at home by failing at work, we're also in trouble. It isn't fair simply to tell parents they need to spend more time with their children when they are faced with ever-increasing demands at work. Somehow we need to make it possible for families to succeed both at home and at work.

Families can't solve these problems alone. We, as a community, have an obligation here. Government can provide some help. I am proud, for example, that the first legislation I signed was the Family and Medical Leave Act, which made it possible for parents to attend to a new baby or a medical emergency without jeopardizing their jobs. I can't begin to tell you how many Americans have stopped to tell me what a difference this has made in their lives. Some 12 million people have taken advantage of that law so far, and a recent bipartisan commission found that nine out of ten companies said it had not hurt their profits.

Our immunization programs, investments in Head Start, and efforts to reduce the chances young people will be involved in crime also have helped families. So has the Earned Income Tax Credit, which cuts taxes of millions of working families with incomes under $28,000 to help keep them out of poverty. The adoption tax credit, which provides a tax credit of up to $5,000 to families with the generosity of spirit to provide a good home to a needy child, has just become law, and will, we all hope, strengthen family life for so many children who need it.

These and other initiatives represent a national recognition of the central role of families in our democratic republic. But as important as these initiatives are, they are just the beginning if we are really going to strengthen families in this time of rapid change. I believe, for example, we need to extend the Family and Medical Leave Act to allow employees to take up to twenty-four hours of unpaid leave a year for parent-teacher conferences and routine medical care for a child. In addition, I support a flex-time initiative that will allow workers to work overtime in exchange for paid time off.

The tax cuts for education and skill development I've proposed will increase substantially opportunities for greater family stability, and we need to make them the law of the land.

Despite the fact that selling tobacco to minors is illegal in every state in the union, the powerful tobacco industry has long targeted advertising and marketing messages to children. We support efforts to make such marketing illegal. Every day 3,000 young people start smoking, and 1,000 of them will eventually die from smoking-related diseases. The tobacco industry has no right to peddle cigarettes to children or encourage them—directly or indirectly—to smoke. It is immoral.

Still, the truth is that government's role in strengthening families, while important, is limited, and all Americans must commit themselves anew to this goal. It takes the unswerving commitment of mothers and fathers, the support of community organizations, the cooperation of caring and responsible businesses, and the assistance of governments at all levels. Just as in the Progressive Era, when people turned to national leaders for help in facing new challenges, so too today it takes national leadership to frame the issues, point the way, and mobilize people to work to resolve them.

The issue of television violence is a good example of how we can all work together to meet this common goal. For many years now, parents across America have been saying there is too much violence and sex on television and clamoring for the government to protect their children from pictures and words that don't belong in the family room. In study after study, evidence has mounted that such imagery is corrosive, numbing, and corrupting. Parents argue they have a right to raise their children in ways that reinforce their values and that adult-content programming is an unwelcome intruder in their homes.

The broadcasters, in turn, say they have rights, too, and argue that government control would violate their constitutionally protected freedom of expression and represents an unwarranted intervention in the free operation of the private marketplace. It is a classic conflict between competing rights in a democracy.

The solution we arrived at—voluntary rating by broadcasters and a small piece of technology called the V-chip that allows parents to screen out objectionable programs—is a perfect example of how Americans can work together to find common ground and solve difficult problems. Government did not force the solution, it enabled it. We passed a law providing for the installation of the V-chip, worked with industry to get them to support it, asked them to do what they could do best—produce and rate programs—then left the decision-making to individual families. We didn't create new regulations for the television industry, we encouraged the industry to regulate itself. We did not take over the role of parents, we handed the remote control back to them equipped with new power and said, in effect, the best programming director for a child is a responsible parent.

With this agreement, private industry's right to create and produce whatever products the marketplace will buy is protected, but balanced by a responsibility to rate the content of its programs so parents know what to screen out. Parents have the right to decent television for their children, but also the responsibility to decide for themselves what is appropriate or not. Government simply suggested the mechanism by which their rights can be protected and their responsibilities met.

That's not the end of the story, though. With the passage of the Telecommunications Act, we have the technology and we have the promise of a ratings system. In the months and years to come, we need to ensure that the promise of a rating system is kept, and just as important, that parents take advantage of the opportunity these agreements have created.

The V-chip is just the first step. We also need more positive programming. Recently, at my urging, the entertainment industry agreed to increase the amount of educational television they produce and broadcast, and to work to change the content of children's television to reduce violence and do a better job of supporting our national values. Just as working together got us an agreement on television violence, it will bring us better children's programming too. Shortly after the second meeting of industry leaders, the FCC approved a new rule requiring three hours a week of network educational programs with widespread support from leaders of the entertainment industry.

More than two centuries ago, Thomas Jefferson argued that the bedrock of American democracy was the "yeoman farmer." And although Jefferson was a farmer himself, he wasn't making a pitch for agriculture. His point was that democracy would rise or fall not on the strength of some political elite, but on the strength of ordinary people who hold a stake in, and take responsibility for, how our society works.

Today, our "yeoman farmers" are America's families. The values they represent, the lessons they pass on to their children, the responsibility they take for shaping their own future, and the dreams they seek to achieve determine much about who we are as a people and what we can become as a nation. But families can be strong only if American democracy provides a climate in which they can thrive. Families can't be strong if they're mired in welfare. They can't be strong if the opportunity to earn a living and support their children is uncertain. They can't achieve economic security unless they have access to education. They can't be strong if the streets in their neighborhoods are dangerous, or if the environment is unsafe, or if events elsewhere in the world seem threatening.

America has a stake in, and a responsibility for, strengthening families, the building blocks of our national community. Families, in turn, have a stake in and a responsibility for strengthening America. That process of strengthening, of taking responsibility, begins in the home, extends into the neighborhood, grows out to the community, and creates a better America.

A critical part of creating a better America is creating stronger communities where America's diversity is respected, even celebrated. This has been a constant challenge for America. It was a century ago when a huge wave of immigrants suffered subtle and not-so-subtle discrimination. Today, America is more diverse than ever. It is amazing to consider that while 197 nations were represented at the Atlanta Olympics, there are people of 150 different racial and ethnic groups in America's largest county! How can we accommodate all the diversity in America and preserve a strong national citizenship? We must begin with the essential proposition that Americans are not bound together by race, religion, or any other single distinguishing trait, but by common allegiance to the Declaration of Independence, the Constitution, and the Bill of Rights, and common embrace of both the privileges and the obligations of citizenship.

I took Latin in high school in Hot Springs, Arkansas, with a wonderful teacher, Mrs. Elizabeth Buck. And as much as I hated learning Latin declensions, it helped me later to understand something important about what America's motto, *E Pluribus Unum,* really means. The Latin in that phrase doesn't mean that we *are* one. It means we are ever striving to *become* one; it's what Lincoln called our "unfinished work."

Our history is full of examples of how hard it has been to create communities that live up to the challenge of our motto. We have had class divisions. We have waged battles against ourselves and wars of conquest against others. We have had religious and ethnic conflicts. We have held prejudices against each wave of immigrants, even though "we" ourselves were often children of immigrants. And, of course, we have struggled with racial conflict from the beginning.

We continue to wrestle with some of these issues today. Racial tensions still divide us. Disagreements over religious expression, especially in school, still flare. And immigration once again is an issue of public debate.

When I was a kid growing up in segregated Arkansas, I rode the city bus to school. It cost a nickel. My friends and I liked to sit at the back of the bus. When the bus was crowded, it was pointed out to us that black folks were supposed to sit in the back of the bus. I didn't know any better. Discrimination doesn't come naturally; it has to be taught.

Martin Luther King, Jr., said that men hate each other because they fear each other. They fear each other because they don't know each other. They don't know each other because they can't communicate with each other. They can't communicate with each other because they're separated from each other. The sad lesson of our experience is that sometimes we can be standing next to one another and still be separated, miles and miles away in our minds.

If we are going to build enduring communities, we have to close that distance. We have to continue to heal the racial divisions that still tear at our nation. We cannot rest until there are no more hate crimes, until there is no more racial violence, and until we have moved beyond those far more subtle but still pervasive racial divisions that keep us from becoming strong communities pulling together as one nation under God. Until we do that, we will not have fulfilled the promise that is America.

We have to be honest about where we are in this struggle. The job of ending discrimination in this country is not over. In Hope, Arkansas, the streets in the black neighborhood near where my grandfather had his store were the only ones in town that weren't paved. The movie house was segregated. The high school from which I graduated was segregated. Thirty years ago it was rare to see women or people of color as police officers or firefighters or doctors or lawyers or college professors or even, believe it or not, sports figures.

The reason that's changing today isn't random historical drift. After all, the Supreme Court rejected the notion that we could ever be separate but equal and Democrats and Republicans alike passed laws against discrimination and created affirmative action programs to redress centuries of wrongs for minorities and women.

Affirmative action was intended to give everybody a fair chance, but it hasn't always worked smoothly and fairly. Today there are those who are determined to put an end to affirmative action, as if the purposes for which it was created have been achieved. They have not. Until they are, we need to mend affirmative action, most certainly, but not end it.

That is exactly what we are trying to do: end abuses, prohibit quotas, subject affirmative action to strict review, oppose any benefits to those who aren't qualified, but make that extra effort to see that everyone has not a guarantee, but a chance.

We are all stronger when everyone has an opportunity to work and serve to the full extent of his or her ability. We can see that clearly in the remarkable record established in our military by minorities and by women who have been made eligible, since I became President, to serve in more than 250,000 new positions. And the public interest has certainly been advanced by the record number of minorities and women appointed to the Cabinet, other important Executive positions, and federal judgeships. We are all better off for their contributions.

We must realize that all Americans, whatever their racial or ethnic origin, share the same old-fashioned values, work hard, care for their families, pay their taxes, and obey the law. We must remember that all Americans are exposed to the problems of crime, drugs, domestic abuse, and teen pregnancy. And we all have a stake in solving these problems together. As Dr. King said, "We must learn to live together as brothers, or we will perish as fools."

This same commitment to tolerance and equal opportunity should govern our approach to immigration. It's important for us all to remember that we are both a nation of immigrants and a nation of laws. Legal immigration has made America what it is today—a vibrant and diverse nation, all the richer for the energy, ideas, and plain hard work immigrants have contributed to our society.

Immigrants who enter our country legally and begin the process of attaining citizenship today are little different from the strivers who were our own ancestors. We need to remember that, and repudiate those who argue against immigration as a thinly veiled pretext for discrimination.

By the same token, we must not tolerate illegal immigration. Since 1992, we have increased our Border Patrol by over 35 percent; deployed underground sensors, infrared night scopes and encrypted radios; built miles of new fences; and installed massive amounts of new lighting. We have moved forcefully to protect American jobs by calling on Congress to enact increased civil and criminal sanctions against employers who hire illegal workers. Since 1993, we have removed over 30,000 illegal workers from jobs across the country. In addition, since January of last year, we have removed more than 50,000 criminal aliens. As I have made clear, I oppose the provisions attached to the welfare reform legislation that deny benefits to legal immigrants. Legal immigrants work, pay taxes, and live up to many other obligations that we owe to one another, and we ought to change those provisions.

I continue to be opposed to welfare benefits for illegal immigrants and believe those family members who sponsor immigrants should be held legally responsible for supporting them. Having said that, I am just as opposed to forcing our teachers to identify the children of illegal immigrants and kick them out of public schools, a mean-spirited and shortsighted effort that, as every major law enforcement organization has said, will only worsen the street crime and gang problem. Finally, the historic political asylum reform we introduced has resulted in a 57 percent reduction in new asylum claims.

If we are to live up to the values embedded in our Constitution, if we are to redeem the promise of America, then we must be one people—white, black, Asian, Latino—not separate camps, but neighbors and fellow citizens who share basic American values and are willing to live by them. Here, on the edge of the twenty-first century, we cannot survive as a divided community.

Like most Americans, my faith has given me strength and comfort throughout my life. It is a private and, in many ways, a conservative faith, in that I believe the government has little place in deeply personal matters.

Ours is a nation founded by people of profound faith. Many of those who came to this new land were searching for a place to express their faith freely without persecution, and our Founders believed that only with Divine guidance could we succeed in confronting the challenges that would face our nation. In fact, they mentioned Divine Providence and the guidance of God twice in the Declaration of Independence. And the First Amendment to our Constitution protects every person's right to freedom of expression, even to freely practice his or her faith without government interference. I am convinced that the strict limits we have placed on government's right to interfere with the free exercise of religion has made us the most religious democracy on Earth. That's why I'm especially proud to have signed in 1993 and to be vigorously enforcing the Religious Freedom Restoration Act, a law that responded to a Supreme Court decision that restricted the exercise of people's religious liberties, by saying that the government has to bend over backwards to avoid limiting people's exercise of their faith, or to place any penalties on doing so.

Americans believe deeply in the need to keep government out of private, personal matters. That is one reason why I am pro-choice. I believe we should all work to reduce the number of abortions. That is why I have worked to reduce teen pregnancy, remove barriers to cross-racial adoption, and provide tax credits to families willing to adopt. Still, I believe the ultimate choice should remain a matter for a woman to decide in consultation with her conscience, her doctor, and her God.

Every great religion teaches honesty, trustworthiness, responsibility, devotion to family, and charity and compassion toward others—the very values we need to build enduring communities. Respect for faith and family and respect for others has helped Americans to work together for more than two centuries. It's made a big difference in the way we live and in our ability to overcome adversity. Mutual respect for different faiths, for different views, has helped keep America strong.

Our Founders understood that religious freedom was basically a coin with two sides. The

Constitution protects the free exercise of religion, but prohibits the establishment of a state religion. It's a careful balance that's uniquely American. It is the genius of the First Amendment. But it does not, as some people have implied, make us a religion-free country. Quite the opposite, in fact.

When the First Amendment is invoked as an obstacle to private expression of religion, it is being misused. Religion has a vital place in community-building because the public square belongs to all Americans. It's especially important that parents feel confident that their children can practice religion. That's why some families have been frustrated to see their children denied even the most private forms of religious expression in public schools.

That is rare, but it has happened and it is wrong. Here is where I stand: I believe the First Amendment does not require students to leave their religion at the schoolhouse door. Just as we wouldn't want students to leave at home the values they learn from religion, we should not require them to refrain from religious expression. Reinforcing those values is an important part of every school's mission, and I've had the U.S. Department of Education issue instructions to all schools accordingly.

I believe the Supreme Court was right a generation ago to prohibit any public authority from creating an official school prayer and making students recite it. But there is absolutely nothing improper about students wanting to reflect upon their faith. Students can pray privately and individually whenever they want. They can express their beliefs in homework, through artwork, and during class presentations, as long as it's relevant to the assignment. They can form religious clubs in high schools.

And even though the schools can't advocate formal religious beliefs, they should teach mainstream values. There are those who say that has no place in public education; I disagree. The violence in our streets is not value-neutral. The movies we see aren't value-neutral. Television is not value-neutral. Too often we see expressions of human degradation, immorality, violence, and debasement of the human soul occupying more space in the minds of our young people than the better values they learn at home. Our schools must be a barricade against this kind of degradation. And we can do it without violating the First Amendment. That's why my administration has done everything it can to promote character education in schools, provide states incentives to develop curricula, and recognize leaders of this movement at the White House. We have got to get this right. America needs to be a place where faith flourishes.

That's never been more important than today, as churches burn in the South. It's hard to think of a more depraved act of hatred than the destruction of a place of worship. Black churches have been the center of worship and community for millions of families across the country. But prejudice and persecution has never succeeded in turning faith to ashes. That's why, standing before the ruins of the Mount Zion AME church in Greeleyville, South Carolina, a year ago, the Reverend Terrence Mackey could turn to his grief-stricken daughter and say, "They didn't burn down the church. They burned down the building in which we hold church. The church is still inside all of us." I was honored, this year, to be able to attend the dedication of Reverend Mackey's new "building."

We must come together, black and white alike, to smother the flames of hatred and kindle the flames of faith and hope. This summer we saw another flame move through the South, toward Atlanta—the flame of the Olympic Torch. It is as old as democracy itself, reaching back through history to Greece and to the wellsprings of what it means yet today to be an American: to believe in liberty, freedom, fair play, a fair chance, mutual respect, honor.

Our communities—our families, our neighborhoods, even our national community—depend on the values, the hope, the belief, the convictions that come with faith, and the sense of security they impart in an uncertain and rapidly changing world.

No discussion of community is complete without a discussion of America's role in the world community. We cannot realize the opportunities of the twenty-first century, or meet its responsibilities, or strengthen our own community, unless we are resolved to remain the world's leading force for peace and freedom, security and prosperity.

I was born exactly half a century ago, as the Second World War ended and the Cold War began. It was a time of great hope, as people rebuilt their lives here at home and as our nation committed itself to rebuilding the war-ravaged economies of Europe and Asia—a commitment that made close friends out of former enemies. But by the time I was in school, it had become a time of looming nuclear peril, an era of "duck and cover" exercises in class and fallout shelters at home. We had a new and singular challenge: an expansionist and hostile Soviet Union that vowed to bury us. And we had a single-minded defense objective: containing that enemy. To achieve that objective, we built sufficient force to deter a Soviet nuclear attack, defend our allies in Europe, and protect our interests in Asia, the Persian Gulf, and elsewhere from Communist aggression.

Today, thanks to the unstinting sacrifice of the American people and our allies, the internal decay of the Soviet system and the courage of those locked within that system, the Cold War is over. Freedom prevailed, the threat of nuclear holocaust was lifted, and people the world over, including the people of the former Soviet Union, were the winners. In this era of unparalleled possibility and hope, democracy is ascendant in more places around the globe than ever before. Free markets are on the rise, as are the standards of living of those who benefit from them.

But while the fall of the Berlin Wall reshaped the world, it did not end its perils or its risks. As long as there are human beings struggling for power and resources, there will be conflict. Ironically, many of the factors which make this a time of great hope—especially, the rapid movement of ideas, information, technology, and people across the borders of open societies—also make us more vulnerable to forces of destruction. The disintegration of the former Soviet Union eliminated the preeminent threat but exposed many others: an increasingly tangled and dangerous web of international terrorism, crime, and drug trafficking; the aggression of rogue states and vicious ethnic and religious conflicts; the spread of dangerous weapons, including nuclear, biological, and chemical ones, and transnational threats like disease, overpopulation, and environmental degradation.

Many of these new threats are as old as civilization itself. They are struggles between the forces of order and disorder, freedom and tyranny, tolerance and repression, hope and fear. They threaten not just peoples and nations, but values and ideas. Just as fascism and then communism attacked the one clear and true idea that defines us and embodies the promise we represent to the world, today's threats attack the idea of a safe and open society of free people.

Despite both the world's enduring tensions and its emerging threats, there are some in both parties who would choose escapism over engagement, who would have us turn inward and ignore our international obligations as the world's oldest democracy. These escapists have waged an all-out assault on the United Nations—even though it can help us share the cost and the risks of engagement. They have slashed our foreign-affairs budget—even though it represents less than two percent of our overall budget. They oppose efforts to open markets and take down barriers to our products through the General Agreement on Tariffs and Trade (GATT) and its successor, the new World Trade Organization, or through the North American Free Trade Agreement (NAFTA), the Summit of the Americas, and the Asia Pacific Economic Council (APEC). In short, they trumpet the rhetoric of American leadership and, at the same time, argue against the commitment of time, energy, and resources that leadership requires.

These escapists are just plain wrong—as wrong as their isolationist predecessors were in the years following the First World War. If we want to meet the challenges and seize the opportunities of this new era, we have to stay engaged. We can't build a wall high enough to keep out the threats to our security—or to isolate ourselves from the world economy, and we can't just go it alone in the world without cooperating with our friends and allies. The global trend toward democracy and free markets is neither inevitable nor irreversible. Our well-being as a nation and our strength as a people depend upon maintaining our leadership abroad. America cannot lead by "escaping," retreating from our responsibilities or our commitments, or going our own way. Instead, we must lead and work with the community of nations.

Like presidents before me, I have taken actions to secure our interests abroad despite opposition at home, knowing that the payoff would come in months or years, not days or weeks. But imagine, for example, what the Persian Gulf would look like today if the United States had not stepped in with our allies in Desert Storm during the Bush administration to stop Iraqi aggression. Imagine the continuing reign of terror and the unchecked flood of refugees to our shores if we had not backed diplomacy with force in Haiti. Imagine the relentless slaughter we would still be seeing in Bosnia had we not brought force to bear there through the North Atlantic Treaty Organization (NATO). Imagine the opportunities and new jobs lost had we not worked hard, Democrats and Republicans alike, to negotiate the removal of trade barriers through GATT and NAFTA. Imagine the flood of illegal immigrants, the lost job opportunities, the increased threat of drug trafficking, had we not given an emergency loan to Mexico when it was in trouble. (By the way, the loan is being paid off ahead of schedule, with interest, and is netting us a nearly $500 million profit.)

To be sure, America cannot be the world's policeman. But we can be the world's peacemaker. We cannot, unilaterally, "make the world safe for democracy," as Woodrow Wilson once believed; but we can help make the world's democracies safe. The global policy choices we make cannot be based upon the budget battles of the moment, or the political whims of the day, or the fear-mongering or demagoguery of a handful of loud isolationist voices. Our choices must be rooted in conviction, stay true to our values, and honor our obligations.

In this era of old and new problems, old and new threats, old and new alignments among and within nations, our goal is constant: to make sure the United States remains the greatest force for peace and prosperity on Earth. When I took office, I said we needed a new strategy to reach that goal as we enter the twenty-first century—a strategy with three parts: first, making the American people more secure by keeping our military and alliances strong to combat the major threats to our security, like the spread of weapons of mass destruction and terrorism. Second, leading the powerful global movement for peace and democracy. And third, creating much greater wealth at home by opening markets abroad.

We've stuck to that strategy—and it's working. Compared to four years ago, our military is stronger, our alliances deeper, and we are facing down the major threats to our security. Conflicts long thought to be unsolvable are closer to resolution. And more markets than ever before are open to American goods and services.

Today, America has the best-trained, best-equipped, and best-prepared fighting force on Earth—and that, more than any other single fact, is the key to our enduring security. We will prefer diplomacy to force, but will always be ready to use military force when necessary to defend our national interests. As we have throughout this century, we will lead with the power of our example, but be prepared, when necessary, to make an example of our power.

Since I came to office, I have kept my pledge to maintain and modernize our defense capabilities. We completed a comprehensive review of our military needs for the future and undertook the most successful restructuring of our forces in history. Even as the size of our forces decreased, their capabilities, readiness, and qualitative edge have increased.

As a result, our military and intelligence forces are more mobile, agile, precise, flexible, smart, and ready than ever before. They are also more coordinated and function more smoothly not only among themselves, but with our allies as well. Today the mere threat of our force can deter would-be aggressors, as we saw recently when we mobilized in the Persian Gulf to counter Saddam Hussein's abortive attempt to mass forces once again at the Kuwaiti border, and then in Haiti, whose dictators finally stepped down when they learned that our armed forces were on their way.

As the world's greatest power and as a leader in the community of nations, we will create, support, and lead alliances of nations and institutions that advance both our national interests and the common interests of our international partners. As we saw in the Gulf War, in Haiti, and now in Bosnia, many other nations who share our goals will also share our burdens—through NATO, the United Nations, in coalitions. The end of the Cold War presented us with an historic opportunity to burnish and broaden our alliances by building a peaceful, undivided, and democratic Europe, and by forging a stable community of nations in a more open and democratic Asia. We have seized it.

In Europe, we have renewed our commitments in NATO—strengthening ties with old friends and, this year, expanding opportunities for our European allies to take the lead in alliance activities when appropriate, and to bear a greater share of our common defense burden. I am proud that America took the lead in opening NATO's door to Europe's newest democracies— first through the Partnership for Peace initiative and soon through enlargement of NATO itself. I believe NATO can and will do for Europe's east what it did for Europe's west fifty years ago: strengthen democracies against future threats, create the conditions for market economies to flourish, and prevent the reemergence of destructive local rivalries. We want NATO to work with Russia and other institutions of European integration to produce what in all Europe's history has never before been more than a dream: a truly united, free Europe.

We have also focused on several regions of special concern. In Russia, for example, we have worked steadily to support the forces of reform as Russia makes its historic transition to a free-market democracy. The recent elections were a stunning achievement—a victory not just for President Boris Yeltsin, but for the forces of reform and democracy. That election demonstrates that Russia's best long-term hope is to continue its struggle to become a stable, democratic, market-oriented nation, secure within its borders and at peace with itself and its neighbors. To the extent that we can help it achieve these objectives, the world will be an infinitely safer place. We have taken the same approach to bolster independence, market reforms, and democracy in Ukraine, the Baltic, the Caucasus, and Central Asia, and throughout Central Europe.

In Asia, our security strategy has four priorities: maintaining our military commitments to the region, supporting stronger security cooperation among Asian nations, providing leadership to combat emerging threats, and supporting emerging democracies. We have worked hard with China to see that it embraces nuclear nonproliferation; agrees to abide by the rules of free and fair trade; cooperates in regional and global security initiatives; and grants basic human rights to its own citizens—in short, to see that a resurgent China takes its rightful place as a leader for positive change for its own people, and for the world.

And we've gotten good results: China cooperated with us in defusing the North Korea nuclear threat, and is supporting our proposal for four-party peace talks with the two Koreas. We have secured China's cooperation on exports of nuclear technology and materials and on a testing ban. In addition, we have enlisted China's support in combating mutual threats like drug trafficking and, more recently, environmental degradation. But we haven't been shy about voicing our differences—and acting on them. When China conducted menacing military exercises in the Taiwan Straits, I sent the Seventh Fleet to the area to demonstrate our commitment to ensuring peaceful relations between China and Taiwan. When China failed to live up to its word to crack down on the pirating of American intellectual property rights like compact discs, we made it clear we would impose sanctions until we got the cooperation that had been promised.

We have taken a firm line with North Korea. North Korea's border with South Korea is the most heavily fortified in the world, and Pyongyang maintains a standing army totaling one million. When I took office, North Korea was several years into a nuclear development program. While parts of that program were perfectly legal, overall there was little question that nuclear weapons development was also an objective. I was determined to stop North Korea's nuclear buildup. So, with the help of our South Korean and Japanese allies and after prolonged negotiations, we secured an agreement that not only froze North Korea's nuclear program, but ensured it would be dismantled under international monitoring. But that is just the beginning. Our long-term objective is the peaceful reunification of the two Koreas, and I am hopeful the four-party peace process we launched will get us closer to that goal.

Our relationship with our partner in the Pacific, Japan, continues to deepen, despite occasional trade disagreements. This spring, after a year-long review, we signed an historic new security accord with Japan and renegotiated our military presence in Okinawa. And we've negotiated twenty-one separate trade agreements, covering everything from computers to medical supplies. As a result, American exports to Japan have increased dramatically—by 85 percent in the sectors covered by the accords. That's meant thousands of new jobs back home in America, and lower prices and greater choice for consumers in Japan. Our partnership with Japan is stronger and more productive for both our people than it has been in years.

A powerful military and strong alliances aren't ends in themselves. We need them to deal with the most basic threats to our security—like the spread of weapons of mass destruction and the challenge of terrorism, international organized crime, and drug trafficking.

When I became President, the dissolution of the Soviet Union created four nuclear powers—Russia, Belarus, Kazakhstan, and Ukraine—where once there had been just one. I saw it as my highest responsibility to continue the work of my predecessors to reduce the threat from Russia and to eliminate it entirely from the other three newly independent states. Today, for the first time in decades, not a single Russian nuclear missile is aimed at an American city. We are cutting Russian and American arsenals by two-thirds from their Cold War height. And soon, there will not be a single nuclear missile left in Ukraine, Belarus, or Kazakhstan.

The irony, of course, is that what made the destruction of nuclear warheads possible—the collapse of the Soviet Union—also increased the potential threat of the theft of nuclear materials and sale of nuclear weapons technology. That's why, with our allies, we are working with Russia and the other newly independent states to strengthen export controls and security at nuclear facilities, remove nuclear materials from insecure sites, stop nuclear theft and smuggling, and reduce the uranium and plutonium available for nuclear weapons. At the same time, we are working to ban the production of material for nuclear weapons, control the transfer of missiles and related technology, and prevent the development of an entirely new generation of nuclear weapons through agreements like the Non-Proliferation Treaty and the Comprehensive Test Ban Treaty.

Despite our extraordinary progress, the fact remains that it only takes a lump of plutonium the size of a soda can to build a bomb, and rogue states are an ever-present threat. It will be more than a decade before any such state will have the ability to launch a long-range missile attack against the continental United States, but in the meantime we must build a sensible national missile defense program. There are some in the Congress who want to revive the recklessly expensive and extreme "Star Wars" scheme—a costly system that is neither necessary nor prudent and that would violate the Anti-Ballistic Missile Treaty. What we need is a practical, smart missile defense program based on real, not theoretical, threats, and that is exactly what we are getting. We're already spending $3 billion a year to develop such a defense by 2000, one that will be deployable by 2003, if needed—well before the threat becomes real. In addition, we are beefing up programs to defend against existing threats such as short- and medium-range missile attacks against our troops and our allies.

While nuclear weapons require fissile materials, advanced technology, and major expenditures of money, chemical and biological weapons do not. And that makes them available to shadowy extremist groups like Aum Supreme Truth, which spread Sarin nerve gas in Tokyo's subway, not just to rogue states like Iraq. Three U.S. administrations have worked with the international community for more than a decade to negotiate a Chemical Weapons Convention. Today it has languished in the Senate, awaiting ratification. We are working hard to negotiate legally binding measures to strengthen the Biological and Toxin Weapons Convention. We cannot limit our vigilance to nuclear weapons; we must move forward with chemical and biological control agreements as well, and quickly.

Keeping America strong and secure also requires standing up to a nexus of new threats: international terrorism, crime, and drugs. These forces of destruction are equal opportunity destroyers with no respect for borders. No one is immune to their danger. Not the people of Japan where a gas attack injured thousands of people. Not the people of Latin America or Southeast Asia where drug traffickers wielding imported weapons have murdered hundreds of innocent people. Not the people of Israel where hatemongers have blown up buses full of children. Not the people of the former Soviet Union and Central Europe where organized criminals are undermining new democracies.

And not the American people. Halfway across the world in Saudi Arabia, nineteen of our finest young men in uniform lost their lives in a cowardly bomb attack while defending our nation's interests. Right here in America, it appears that homegrown terrorists blew up the Murrah Federal Building while foreign terrorists tried to topple the World Trade Center. And drug traffickers poison our children and breed violence in our streets.

These forces of destruction never give up; but we will never give in. And with ironclad determination, steadiness, and resolve, we will defeat them. I intend to continue to push hard to make sure that our anti-terrorism tools include the strongest possible provisions.

We are pursuing a three-part strategy against terrorism.

First, we're rallying the world community to stand with us. From the Summit of the Peacemakers in Sharm el-Sheikh, Egypt, where thirteen Arab nations for the first time condemned terror in Israel and throughout the Mideast, to the anti-terror agreements we recently reached with our G-7 partners and Russia to take specific common actions to fight terrorism.

We are moving forward together. Our intelligence services have been sharing more information with other nations than ever to stop terrorists before they act, capture them if they do, and see that they're brought to justice. We've imposed stiff sanctions with our allies against states that support terrorists. When necessary, we're acting on our own. A law I signed in the summer of 1995 will help to deny Iran and Libya the money they use to finance international terrorism.

Second, our anti-terrorism strategy relies on tough enforcement and stern punishment here at home. We made terrorism a federal offense, expanded the role of the FBI, enacted the death penalty. We've hired more law enforcement personnel, added resources, improved training. And I'm proposing a new law that will help to keep terrorists off our soil, fight money laundering, and punish violent crimes committed against Americans abroad.

Third, we're tightening security on our airplanes and at our nation's airports. From now on we'll hand-search more luggage and screen more bags and require preflight inspections for any plane flying to or from the United States. I've asked Vice President Gore to head an effort to deploy new high-technology inspection machines at our airports and to review all our security operations.

Law enforcement has asked for wiretap authority to enable them to follow terrorists as they move from phone to phone. This is the only way to track stealthy terrorists as they plot their crimes. This authority has already been granted to our law enforcement officials when they're dealing with organized criminals. Surely it is even more urgent to give them this authority when it comes to terrorists. But Congress said no.

And law enforcement has also asked that explosives used to make a bomb be marked with a taggant, a trace chemical or microscopic plastic chip scattered throughout the explosives. This way sophisticated machines can find bombs before they explode, and when they do explode, police scientists can trace a bomb back to the people who actually sold the explosive materials that led to the bomb.

Congress said no to this too, although tagging works. In Switzerland over the past decade it has helped to identify who made bombs and explosives in over 500 cases. When it was being tested in our country several years ago, it helped police find a murderer in Maryland. We need these tough tools so that we can continue to crack down on terrorism here and abroad.

Much of this work by law enforcement, intelligence and military professionals goes unheralded, but we are getting results. For example, we prevented attacks on the United Nations and the Holland Tunnel in New York. We thwarted an attempt to bomb American passenger planes from the skies over the Pacific. We convicted those responsible for the World Trade Center bombing and arrested suspects in the Oklahoma City and Unabomber cases. We've tracked down terrorists around the world and brought them to justice in America. We can whip this problem.

Just as no enemy could drive us from the fight to meet our challenges and protect our values in the Second World War and the Cold War, we cannot be driven from the fight against today's enemy—terrorism. We know that if we all work together, we will prevail.

We're also cooperating worldwide to increase drug enforcement information-sharing, shut down front companies and money-laundering operations, crack down on drug-related corruption, and to provide military support to stem the international trade in drugs.

Some transnational problems pose less immediate, but no less dangerous, threats to our security. We're fighting frightening new diseases worldwide, supporting sustainable development in areas of the globe where population pressures have stripped the earth of resources, fighting famine with food aid and agricultural assistance, and combating resource scarcities with new technologies. We're leading the way to protect the world's fisheries, ban ocean dumping of radioactive materials, and end the use of chemicals that endanger species and human lives or damage the atmosphere's ozone layer. Anyone who sees famine as only an agricultural issue, or crowded cities as only a population issue, or water shortages as only an environmental issue, has no understanding of the sometimes violent sweep of human history. Eventually, left untended, such issues can become national security issues.

America also has a special role to play in defending and expanding the community of democratic nations and being an active force for peace in a world still wracked by conflict. Nothing will strengthen our own security more in the long run. When people live free and at peace, they're less likely to resort to violence to settle their problems or to abuse the rights of their fellow citizens. They're more likely to be good trading partners and to join with us to conquer common problems. We can see this so clearly in our own hemisphere, where the powerful movement to democracy has produced unparalleled cooperation in opening markets and in dealing with drugs and illegal immigrants.

Democracy does not come easily, cheaply, or quickly. As our own history demonstrates, democracies are built slowly, not all at once. History also tells us that countries making the transition from authoritarian regimes to democracy are unstable and prone to conflict, especially if they are not also making economic progress.

So our commitment to the peaceful resolution of the world's conflicts, and our investment in building democracy, must remain steady and strong. The payoffs are priceless. Through our patient diplomacy, our willingness to underwrite reasonable risk-taking, and the courage—despite assassin bullets and terrorist bombs—of Israeli, Palestinian, and Arab leaders, we are closer today to peace in the Mideast than ever before. Partly because of our help, there is hope for peace in Northern Ireland. In Haiti, our military task complete, we are working to help the Haitians help themselves to live free of fear and poverty. And in Bosnia—after the worst atrocities in Europe since the Second World War—American troops and their counterparts from many nations have stopped the snipers and shells. Now, they are helping the people of Bosnia rebuild their lives and their land in peace.

In this new era, we must never forget that the true measure of our people's security includes not only their physical safety, but their economic well-being, too. Decades from now, I believe people will look back at this period and see the most far-reaching changes in the world trading system in generations—changes that are making a dramatic difference in the lives of the American people. As I have described, through GATT and NAFTA—and through hard-headed persuasion like our work with Japan on auto parts—barriers to American products have come down and our exports have reached a record high, creating more than one million new jobs in the last four years alone. I want us to continue to turn our vision of open markets throughout the Asia Pacific region—the fastest-growing region in the world—into a practical reality. And we should continue to extend the reach of free and fair trade on every continent—especially to our neighbors in the Americas. We have the best workers and the best products in the world. Give them a fair deal with free trade and they will bring even greater prosperity home to America, and help the world to grow faster as well.

The world looks to America for leadership not just because of our size and strength, but because of what we stand for and what we have the courage to stand against. We are, as we long have been, a beacon for freedom, a bastion for democracy, a living example of the promise of liberty for people throughout the world. Just as an individual in a community has both opportunities and responsibilities, so too does a nation in the community of nations. If what we seek are the opportunities presented by a world that is at peace, then we must shoulder our responsibilities to that world, not give it the cold shoulder. Where alliances are required, we must forge them. Where negotiation is required, we must undertake it. Where investment is required, we must make it. And where force is required to secure our interests, we must use it.

We must welcome the world's hope and trust, not shy away from it—not just for the world, but for ourselves.

In a world that technology makes smaller every day, it is no longer possible to separate neatly the issues of community that affect only our families, only our neighborhoods, only our nation. The global village is no longer a futuristic phrase, it is a practical, daily reality. Our children wear clothes and listen to music from around the world; some of them even communicate with "electronic pen pals" via the Internet. Our neighborhood stores are stocked with products as likely to be produced in Malaysia as in Minneapolis. The company we work for is more and more likely these days to have customers in Asia or Africa as in America, and indeed may well be a subsidiary of a larger company headquartered elsewhere in the world.

This increasing international interdependence is seen by some as a threat to our nation and our values as Americans—but the truth is almost precisely the reverse. It is American values and principles—freedom, self-determination, market economies—that are ascendant around the globe. It is American companies that are gaining most from the rapid growth in international trade. It is American products made by American workers that are in highest demand as the standards of living improve in countries around the world.

We are connected in a myriad of ways not just to the neighbors in our own community, but to neighbors in communities the world over. As we move into a new century, those connections will only increase, and as they do, we will be enriched. It is not a future we should flee from, but one we must embrace together wholeheartedly—guided by the principles upon which our nation was founded, certain of the values which have made us strong, and confident of our ability to seize the opportunities and shoulder the responsibilities that future will present us.

Conclusion

I WANT TO END THIS BOOK BY RETURNING TO the beginning, to Marilyn Concepción, that AmeriCorps member from Providence, Rhode Island. Here is a young woman, an immigrant to our shores, who was given an opportunity and seized it, who took responsibility for her own future, and who has devoted herself to the service of her community.

Ms. Concepción is a symbol of the promise of America, and AmeriCorps is a metaphor for what it takes to renew that promise today for all Americans: the promise of opportunity, the obligation of responsibility, and the duty to community.

AmeriCorps, the program that provided Ms. Concepción with her first opportunity, has been under attack by some self-styled conservatives virtually from the day it was created. Yet it has provided these opportunities to some 45,000 young Americans. And it embodies both the core values that have made our nation great and the choice I believe Americans must make about our future. Do we want a nation that supports the principles and values of our Founders, the same principles and values we have struggled to uphold for more than two centuries and that AmeriCorps stands for today? Or do we want an America that reneges on its promise of opportunity, that shirks its responsibilities, and that divides, rather than unites, our American community?

Nothing so clearly illustrates this choice than the budget battle of the last year; nothing demonstrates more clearly what is at stake today. Ultimately, the budget battle was not a disagreement about whether we should balance the budget. My plan and Congress's plan both did that. The battle was about whether, as a nation, we would honor our obligations to our families, to our children, to our parents and grandparents, and to future generations. It was about whether we would make the investments in education, in the environment, and in Medicare and Medicaid that enable us to meet those obligations. It was, quite simply, about whether we would continue to live by our core values—opportunity, responsibility, community—or abandon them.

There is an old hymn that says, "Once to every man and nation, comes the moment to decide." In fact, over the course of our history, there have been many such moments: when we made the fateful decision to declare our nationhood, when we fought each other in a Civil War to preserve the Union and end slavery, when we renewed our basic principles and values in the face of a new Industrial Age that seemed to throw them into question, when we fought and helped win two world wars abroad, when we defeated the Great Depression and opened the door to prosperity here at home, and when we struggled against a mighty enemy to contain communism in the Cold War.

Now, I believe with all my heart, this is another moment for Americans to decide. Here, at the edge of a new century, we must decide between two visions of America. One vision foresees an "every man for himself," "you're on your own" America. This vision pays lip service to the importance of individual effort and strong families without assuring individuals and families the tools they need to succeed. This vision divides rather than unites us. This vision trumpets America's leadership in the world without supporting the policies necessary to maintain it. This vision often demonizes the people's government and is bereft of the simple understanding that in America we must go forward together, and we don't have a single person to waste.

This vision will not give us the America I want in the year 2000—an America in which all responsible citizens have a chance to live their dreams, an America growing together, an America leading the world to greater peace, freedom, and prosperity.

I have a different vision of our future, one that is grounded in our founding principles and in the values that have made us great, a vision that will draw us together, not pull us apart. My vision does not seek to promote government but to perfect it, to make it a better servant of our people. It doesn't seek to demean the free marketplace, but to strengthen it and to take account of what it cannot be expected to do. It does not promise a future of perfection, but it does provide a path of progress.

For mine is a truly progressive vision of the future, one that traces a continuous arc from the principles of our Founders to our prospects in the next century. The components of this vision are straightforward. They include many of the practical proposals I have made in this book, involving work that still needs to be done. For example, we must invest in our people today so they can succeed tomorrow with initiatives like our Hope Scholarships that will throw open the doors of college even wider. We must help more people to be both good parents and good workers by, among other things, expanding the Family Medical Leave Act. We must help make our people safer by, for instance, banning cop-killer bullets that threaten the police who protect us. And we must finish the job of implementing real welfare reform that truly moves people from dependence to independence, and that is good for our children.

Beyond these measures, and more, we must make sure that we do not turn back from the progress we have made in such areas as our efforts to limit the tobacco industry's ability to appeal to our youth; our plan to finish putting 100,000 police officers on our streets; our gains in environmental protection; and our ability to give people a chance to serve their communities and help themselves through AmeriCorps.

If we continue to follow the opportunity-responsibility-community strategy which has brought us so far, we will build an America that is leading the world to greater peace and freedom and prosperity, an America coming together on the strength of our marvelous diversity, an America where all our children, wherever they start in life, will have the chance to live their dreams.

Last year, my wife Hillary wrote a book about children that borrowed its title from an old African saying that "it takes a village to raise a child." As I conclude this book, it occurs to me that it is really about what it takes to make a village.

We can build that village. We can beat back the forces of division and cynicism and reinvigorate our national community. We must believe we can. Whenever we grow weary and doubtful, we should remember how the rest of the world sees us. America stands as a beacon of freedom, opportunity, and peace across the globe, as I heard again and again in my visits with Olympic athletes from other lands: from the Mideast to South Africa, from the former Soviet republics to Bosnia and Northern Ireland.

When I visited Ireland last year, I met with Seamus Heaney, the Nobel Prize–winning poet, a man who has chronicled Ireland's long struggle and his own fight against cynicism and defeat. I was particularly moved by some words he had written, which I quoted in my speeches to the Irish people. Later, he was kind enough to write them out for me. That piece of paper now hangs in my study in the White House, and I look at it often. One line always leaps out at me—the moment when "hope and history rhyme."

I believe that America today stands between hope and history—at the edge of a moment when these two powerful forces are as one, when we can embrace the dawn of the new century, drawing strength and guidance from our past, filled with confidence that in this new age of possibility, our best is yet to come.

Acknowledgments

This book grew out of countless discussions with men and women from all walks of life over the past several years. I especially want to thank all those people with whom I have worked in public life to develop and implement many of the ideas in this book. My vision for the challenges America faces as it prepares to enter the twenty-first century was immeasurably enriched as a result. I am grateful to each and every one who took time to share with me their thoughts about how this great nation of ours can continue to grow and prosper.

I could not have written this book without the support and ideas, the experience and wisdom of Vice President Al Gore, and my wife, Hillary. I thank them both.

I particularly want to acknowledge author and public policy consultant William E. Nothdurft, who was primarily responsible for helping to draft this book, and Joellyn Murphy, his researcher. Their professionalism, skill, and diligence benefited the book at every stage.

Eli Segal was instrumental in making this book possible, and I am, as ever, grateful for his continuing friendship.

Finally, I want to thank the entire team at Times Books, especially Peter Osnos, its publisher, and Steve Wasserman, its editorial director, for their enthusiasm and persistence.